One
Live It

Carole Fortune

DEDICATION

I dedicate this book to my children Jade and Ryan Fortune
who have wholeheartedly supported me with my events
and the road to recovery. Thank you both.

CONTENTS

Introduction

ACKNOWLEDGMENTS

I would like to thank my many many running friends who over the years have participated in races and trained with me. Their camaraderie, putting up with my dedication and motivation whilst showing no compassion. Some have been mentioned throughout the book too many to acknowledge individually.

Further reading on the history of the Pentland Hills can be found in 'The Pentland Hills' by Jim Crumley

Introduction

This is not a dialogue of heroes or heroines it is just a simple personal memoir of an obsession of running with resilience to overcome pain, injuries or accidents. A mindset to conquer whatever life throws at you regardless of the degree.

I have always been interested in exercise in some format from school years when I was a member of Edinburgh Southern Harriers training at Meadowbank Stadium in Edinburgh. I went on to join The Edinburgh Health Club where I started bodybuilding which I thoroughly enjoyed developing muscles. Alas I am no mesomorph and I struggled to build noticeable muscle mass, but I was content with muscle definition.

I took up Karate for a short while just before Aerobic exercise boom in the 90's. Of course, that was next on the list and I trained to be an Aerobics Instructor and a Personal Trainer. Alas, I let the teaching dissipate as I did not maintain my CPD (Continuing Professional

Development) training, on the other hand it gave me a valuable knowledge of exercise and the body.

I have experienced the joy of running in Park Runs, Marathons, Ultra-marathons, Triathlons, Duathlons and Ironman events, experiencing countless injuries and accidents along the way. This memoir encounters those experiences, with the odd moment or two of competitive glory to treasure, I have endured two brink of death threats and overcome both.

I have only ever won one race in 2006, 1st Female, the Oban Half Marathon and placed 2nd Female in a Marathon, the Moray Marathon 2006. When runners exchange stories you can see it in their eyes the love of this sport.

I go through phases of which type of sporting events I like the best and currently its Hill Racing that attracts my attention, I love running and I love running in the hills. I have the Pentland Hills on my doorstep, how privileged am I to have such beauty to explore.

Running – It's just something I do! take it up – if you want fun and fulfilment!!

1 IN THE BEGINNING IT WAS MARATHONS

I have never counted the amount of Marathons I have run but I am on my way to 40, I think, one day I must count. There are some marathons that hold a special place, London has to be one of them I have run 15 in total. I was supposed to run my 16th in April 2020 but it was cancelled thanks to Covid-19.

I spent a few years living in Cairo and got involved with a group of runners. We would meet at the track at the Cairo American Campus (CAC) at 05:00 to run before the dust, dogs, the sun and the masses of people got up. I had just started running so I was running only about three miles alternative mornings around the track. A group of regular runners at the track were in training for the Luxor marathon and they asked me if I would like to join them. I started going out with them on their weekly long run which could be anything from running up to the Mocatam (mountains) or to the Pyramids at Giza or Sakhara. We would leave extra early at 4:30am before sunrise with handfuls of rocks to ward off the Beladi (stray) dogs who would bark and chase you down the road in packs.

This led to my first marathon in Luxor 2008 where 500 runners from twenty-seven different countries took part in the 25th edition of the Egyptian International Marathon. The starting line was at the 3,500-year-old Mortuary Temple of Hatshepsut and the race finished at the Kings and Queens Valleys in Luxor. The runners passed by the Dynasty XVIII-era Colossi of Memnon statues, Al-Sayeda Zainab Mosque, Qarana Hospital and the area of the Pharaonic Valleys, and then returned to the starting line at Hatshepsut Temple. The race was organized by the Ministry of Tourism in cooperation with the Ministry of Interior and the Luxor governor. The Egyptian marathon has been held annually since 1994 as a way to boost tourism in Luxor. The Temple of Hatshepsut was chosen to be the starting point for the marathon because of its inspirational drawings on the temple and surrounds. Although I had built up the runs I had been doing, I only had a short period of time to build up to marathon fitness, based on running only three miles on alternative day to running a marathon in 6 months, not recommended as I suffered immensely from lack of endurance training. A young boy came running towards me near the finish to cheer me on, his father pulled him away saying "sibyha heyya tabana" (leave her, she's tired). The sunglasses shielded the tears of pain as I crossed the finish line in 4:17 vowing never to run a marathon again.

' Ma'di Wadi Runners'

The same group, Ma'adi Wadi Runners, had
entered the Malta Marathon 1999 so after a
few weeks recovery I convinced myself it
wasn't that painful and I had time to train for a
marathon this time. The Malta Marathon starts
from outside Mdina and finish in Sliema with a
drop of 200 metres from start to finish. I ran
comfortably this time finishing in 3 hrs 30
placing 6th Female securing 2nd Age Group
0/35, we also secured 2nd team prize, Percy
Dunn part our group won the race in 2hrs 26.
This is where my interest in Marathon running
started when I realised I wasn't that bad at
marathon running after all!

1999 my next marathon was The Edinburgh Marathon which then started in Dunfermline and you ran over the Forth Road Bridge, finishing in a similar time to Malta in 3:35, the Edinburgh Evening New headlines 'Ups and downs of killer course'. Edinburgh Marathon is now flat and fast with the course voted the fastest marathon in the UK by Runners World, perfect if you are looking for a PB and is the second largest marathon in the UK, behind London.

I got into London with my first ballot entry attempt in 2001 when it was Flora London, Marathon, since then I have qualified for a Good for Age Place every year with one year securing a Championship Place.

I started to choose Marathons in cities abroad that I would like to visit so it was Paris Marathon in 2002 as a family trip meeting friends over there. On the morning of the race we took the metro to the Arc De Triomphe in the bright sunshine. The weather was glorious, a cool breeze and clear skies so different from the freezing temperatures and biting winds of the UK. The Champs-Élysées was packed with people but it didn't feel too crowded. The race weaves around stunning buildings past Le Louvre museum. The support was amazing with people shouting 'Allez Allez!' and waving banners. The route passes all the famous sights such as The Eifel Tower and running through two different forests. There are some great gentle downhill sections through tunnels. These were immense fun because it was a brief respite from the blazing sun and they were all dressed up like a nightclub with lights and music. Similar finish time 3:32:04

A group of running friends headed to Amsterdam Marathon looking forward to a flat course with only 54m of elevation over the whole route starting and finishing in the Olympic stadium. The atmosphere was reaching a crescendo as the Dutch commentator hyped up the crowd and the music was turned up full blast. An amazing backdrop to start a marathon. The route hugged the Amstel River as barges with rather large speakers on banged out some European pop belters and the odd techno smasher. Finished a bit slower this time 3:42 I remember it being bitterly cold and a nice flat course no excuse for being slower, you get out a race what you put into the training.

It was 2004 that I won (1st Female) my one and only race, Oban Half Marathon, 1:37:02, not exactly a record-breaking time which demonstrates it depends strictly on who is in the race, hence the expression 'you've got to be in it to win it'! I was also 1st vet and was presented with two prizes much to the delight of myself but not the locals!

2005 I was 3rd female in the Edinburgh to North Berwick road race and as I crossed the finish line the commentator announced "Carole Fortune, 3rd female unaffiliated, can you imagine how well she would do if she was in a running club". I was at the race with my friend Ruth who was in Gala Harriers, a Scottish Borders running club, I mulled on joining with respect to my father being born and bred in the Borders, Heriot. I have been a member of Gala Harriers since, except from a few years where I was affiliated to a Triathlon Club, Edinburgh Triathletes, when my main sport was triathlons.

When I ceased taking part in Triathlons I went back to running, I joined a running club based in the West of the Pentland Hills to get to know the Southern area of the Pentlands that I was not too familiar with. The Club kept records of Male and Female Best performances in five-year age bands for marathons, Half marathons, 10K and 5K. I had broken the majority of their Age Group performance records, for my age at the time, and I was enjoying breaking my own records. In 2018 I met a running buddy from Gala Harrier I had not seen in years and she managed to convince me to re-join Gala Harriers, I had missed the camaraderie with my Gala running buddies. Gala Harriers were my first claim club with Scottish Athletics and I started to compete in the winter Cross Country races representing them, the other running club questioned this. My records were expunged after a meeting to discuss how can a member who has another club as first claim take part in their club recreation events, many backed me but it was overruled therefore, I expunged myself from their club but had met a lot of new running friends I am still in touch with.

2006 was a particularly busy year for marathon running and in March my group of running friends went to Rome as we liked the sound of "Run Rome the Marathon" it is like running in an open-air museum! Rome is a unique city, full of charm and surprises. The Marathon passed some of the most incredible sights, following the steps of Roman gladiators as well as those of hundreds of thousands of marathoners. The race starts and finishes at the Colosseum where after the Italian anthem is sung, the wheelchairs and faster runners are released onto the start on cobblestones. The route then tours Rome, including some of the non-touristy areas and passes by the Vatican City. There is a lot of cobblestones in the last few miles, with the Piazza Navona and the Piazza del Popolo with many spectators and tourists. 3:27:21 was my finish time.

Rome served as good training for London marathon in April where I got a faster result 3:15:55, 245th Female and 70th F40-49 It was then I realised a sub 3:15 time qualified me for a championship place in the London Marathon. I then went on to run the Edinburgh Marathon in 3:18:19, placing 2nd F40-44. I was determined to get a sub 3hr 15 for this place so I chose not to engage brain and ease off with marathon running, but to force myself on.

Moray Marathon is the oldest running marathon in Scotland, the first Moray Marathon was held in 1982 and developed into a 3 in 1 running event incorporating the Marathon, Half Marathon and 10K Road Races. What better place is there than home turf, North Scotland, to have a try at the qualifying time. The 2006 event celebrated the 25th anniversary of the marathon with Simon

Pride (Forres Harriers) finishing in 2:39:53 to win the event for the 5th time and Kate Jenkins (Gala Harriers) first woman home in 2:58:29 to win her 8th Moray Marathon In the last mile leading to the finish time I was aware of the time and I had to keep pushing myself, to achieve the sub 3:15; it became more a psychological challenge than a physical one, almost talking to myself out loud, you can do it, I only just scraped it with 20 seconds to spare but championship place secured. Results:

1 *Simon Pride Forres 2.39.53*
2 *Alan Reid Peterhead 2.51.05*
3 *John Kennedy Clydesdale 2.53.18*
8 *(1F) Kate Jenkins Gala 2.58.29*
20 *(2F) Carole Fortune Gala 3.14.40*
26 *(3F) Dawn Hardy Moray 3.19.36*

Now that I had secured my qualifying time I could 'relax' a little but I still had another two marathons in that year to run. In October, it was The Loch Ness Marathon with its spectacular scenery and where you learnt what the word undulating means. The Marathon starts on the high ground between Fort Augustus and Foyers and drops down to the banks of Loch Ness. The route follows the Loch's South Eastern shore, heading north east towards Dores on the northern tip of the loch and heads directly into the centre of Inverness turning left over the main road bridge for the last half mile along the River Ness to the finish at Bught Park in the centre of Inverness. Finish time was 3:18:33, 10th Female and 1st Age Group.

The final marathon of 2006 was The New York City Marathon, my group of running buddies had secured places and we headed to the Big Apple for this famous marathon. That year myself and a close friend, Bill Lumsden, ran these six marathons from April – November with me. The New York City Marathon is the largest marathon in the world, that runs through the five boroughs of New York City; it is an awesome experience. The course is a little less than flat with all the bridges. Very late in the season. The winning time is a bit slower than all other city marathons, New York 2:08 seems to be the limit. Both the men and the women's races had unpredictable events and it made for exciting viewing in each race! Lining up it seemed a forgone conclusion that Paula Radcliffe would win easily by halfway and then finish off any hangers on in the last 10 km. On the men's side seasoned vets like Gharib and Cheruiyot were pegged to take the win with Ryan Hall posting another good result after

Martin Lel pulled out.

Paula was setting the pace at the start for the women's race, although it was not particularly fast. A fall from Salina Kosgei in the fourth mile, she went down, apparently tripping on her own feet, then another casualty, Yuri Kano, hit the deck hard. Kosgei fought back and hung on to finish a respectable 5th, while Kano was probably more impressive with her 9th place after what looked like a very hard fall. Radcliffe was gone, recovering from minor surgery to her foot and it was Tulu who was sitting in and waiting for the final stretch before winning by eight seconds in 2:28:52.

The men's race was similar with Martin Lel the hot favorite but he pulled out, Boston King Cheriyot was the next in line, although he has been plagued with injuries and then Kwambai for the first half they were never below 2:10 pace, which explained the massive group of 18 men that stayed together through halfway. The pace went from about 5:00 per mile to 4:42 for mile 17 and 4:39 for mile 18. Gharib was the first to get dropped, although he clawed back to finish third, and by mile 22 it was Meb vs. Cheruiyot. Meb turned on the jets with just over two miles to go, surging and getting a meaningful gap on the Kenyan. He opened up a 41 second margin over those remaining miles, giving him enough of a lead to savour the victory and be the only one in the photo crossing the line in first.

As excited as I was by the racing the New York Marathon with Paula Radcliffe on the start line, I was not convinced I was going to run another sub 3:15. NYC is unique among the big city marathons—London, Berlin, Chicago, and even Boston are fast courses that tend to be won by the "fastest" runners setting their suicidal paces.

On the morning of the marathon you are bussed out to the starting village located on Staten Island. It was absolutely baltic and with over an hour to wait we had to huddle together for warmth. The race starts on the Verrazzano-Narrow Bridge, Staten Island and takes runners through Brooklyn, then into Queens, before entering Manhattan. After a trip up into the Bronx, runners head back down into Manhattan and enter Central Park. Six marathons in one year and starting to feel it hence I was starting to slow down and finished in 3:24:14, 303 out of 12,321 females.

2007 April Flora London Marathon, Championship race came around. The day before the marathon we took the train down to London and straight to the London Expo Centre to collect our race numbers and kit bags and then the excitement kicked in that I was going to run the London Marathon with the elite runners.

Early next morning thanks to Transport for London and Southeastern marathon runners enjoy free travel with smiling staff to get us to Greenwich on time to the start line. We arrived at Greenwich in good time and enjoyed the atmosphere with the sun already shining strongly from the outset and temperature was set to rise above 20C. My London Marathon buddy of several years, Bill, accompanied me to the start area, who had also run the six marathons with me in the lead up to securing my Championship place. He wished me luck as I went into the upmarket toilets that are laid on for Elite runners and he went to join the mass field that started slightly later than us. Any doubts of standing on the start line with the Elite runners, knowing I wasn't good enough to be with them soon faded as we were called to

the start line. Let the magical experience begin.
I had not done a lot of intense training but there
I was on the start line with the Female Elite
runners, no Paula Radcliffe this year but I
recognised a few of the faces, Liz Yelling, Liz
Hawker, Liz McColgan and Gete Wami. As the
television cameras came round introducing all
the potential winners there, I was smiling away
savouring the moment of being on an elite start
line. There was the car with a race timer clock
on it for us to follow, gun goes and for about
the first three miles I had other runners around
me but as elite runners are a lot faster than me
they soon disappeared and I ran the London
Marathon with only a few others beside me.
The course is flat and fast starting in
Blackheath, heads east through Charlton and
Woolwich for three miles, turns west and
passes the Cutty Sark in Greenwich after six to
seven miles. The Elite men start 30mins after
us and it wasn't long before the car with the
race clock and the Elite men ran past me, that
was an amazing experience to be so close to
those international runners, that mile was my
fastest mile as adrenalin surged. At around 13
miles as the route crosses over The Tower
Bridge on the other side of the road other
runners are approaching twenty-three. When I
reach this stage of 23 miles, I am having to

draw on both my physical and psychological
reserves – it is as much in the head as in the
body at this stage. I must have been looking
drained, my number was 202, I heard a lady in
the crowd shout to me '202 I'm backing you',
which I did find amusing. As I was
approaching the finish towards Parliament
Square and going down Birdcage Walk with
the distance markers starting to proclaim
600m, then 400m and finally 200m to go. I took
one last look at my watch and saw that with a
strong finish I could secure at least 3:25 so I
surged my body one last time to push for the
end and crossed the line in 3:25, securing my
Good for Age place for next year. It was a once
in a lifetime experience.

Paula Radcliffe was away for the second year
running, Chunxiu Zhou became the first
Chinese woman to win the Flora London
Marathon 2007– or any World Marathon Major
– and her strong finish offered a glimpse of
what might come from the home team at the
Beijing Olympics next year. She said " For the
first 30km I was just following other people
then I was trying to the best of my ability and
ran fast. I think if the weather was colder, I
could achieve better results." In second place,
Gete Wami, Constantina Dita came third but

admitted that, like thousands of other runners, she suffered in the conditions while Liz Yelling also reached the top 10 and qualified for next year's Olympics, finishing eighth in 2:30.

There were two very familiar faces at the front of the men's race, though. The 2005 Flora London Marathon winner, Martin Lel, snatched the title back from fellow Kenyan Felix Limo. Limo finished third-place finish this year behind, the Moroccan Abderrahim Goumri – finished his debut marathon in style just three seconds behind the leader. Further down the field Ryan Hall ran an impressive 2:08:24, setting a new American record for a debut marathon. Dan Robinson was the first British man and was pleased with his performance, while Haile Gebrselassie had another FLM disappointment, pulling out at 20 miles with a stitch.

The Edinburgh Marathon was becoming a regular on the yearly marathon calendar, I took part in it at least seven times. The first Edinburgh Marathon was in 1982 with further marathons held in 1986 and 1999. They restarted in 2003 with the current route beginning in the city centre, heading out of Edinburgh into East Lothian, finishing at Musselburgh, East Lothian

The first time I ran the Edinburgh Marathon it started in Dunfermline where you ran over the Forth Road Bridge along South Queensferry ending in Meadowbank Stadium which is currently under redevelopment. The route since then has changed a few times, since 2003, it now boasts a route which showcases the incredible and stunning historic city of Edinburgh at its best but also stays true to its worldwide reputation as one of the fastest marathon routes approved by an IAAF label.

It has become a large attraction now named "The Edinburgh Marathon Festival" which annually attracts more than 30,000 runners each year has had an economic impact in the region of £40 million for Scotland's capital and helped raise more than £60 million for various charities. The Edinburgh Marathon joined the world's elite road races in 2012 by becoming the first race in Scotland to be officially recognised by the IAAF, the athletics governing body.

The course has a descent of almost 90 metres to near sea level, boasting it as one of, if not, the fastest marathon routes in the world. If you put in the training then this route can reward you with a PB. Second only to London in terms of size in the UK, the Edinburgh Marathon Festival has eight races in total over the weekend with a 10K, 5K and two junior races on the Saturday and on the Sunday, the

Edinburgh Marathon, Edinburgh Half Marathon and team relay start from the heart of Edinburgh City at Potterrow. The route passes Greyfriars Bobby, down the High Street onto the Mound into Princes Street, with the iconic Edinburgh Castle as the backdrop. The route then takes in the 'Gothic Rocket', otherwise known as the Scott Monument, then it's down the historic Royal Mile, heading towards and past Scottish Parliament building. Here you can look up and view the Arthurs Seat & Salisbury Crags, as well as the Palace of Holyrood, before exiting the Royal Park and heading east towards the coast. As you reach Musselburgh, you run past the oldest golf course in the world, where it's documented that golf has been played as early as 1672, then head further to the East on the flat to Gosford House, an imposing neo-classical mansion which was one of the last great architectural commissions of the celebrated Scots architect, Robert Adam. This is where you turn and head back along the coast, usually with a strong head wind but you'll know the finish line is close, one of the best sights for any marathon runner! With a descent of almost 90 metres to near sea level, bask in the glory of that new PB!

The AYE Club is an informal group of runners who have completed all of the current series of the Edinburgh Marathon (2003 onward). A friend of mine, Chris Burns, had the pleasure of meeting me for the first time with my skull bone exposed, which I will explain later, is the president of the AYE club. I was invited to dinner as the guest of honour to present a talk in 2016. I received an "AYE 2016" memento which was individually engraved on unique sea glass which was collected over the years on beaches at Applecross and North Berwick. They are titled 2016 as that's the year they were issued to the 'Class of 2015'. A unique gesture by Chris who said "my engraving skills are not brilliant but I was seeking something as unique as each individual runner".

My talk was to be an inspirational talk on how I overcame a death-defying accident in 2009 whilst I was out cycling. Chris started the talk for me with a very flattering introduction on how I fought back and continued with my sporting ventures!

AYE 2016 memento sea glass

Members of the AYE Club 2016

*"Annual dinner on Friday night was a huge
success and we were honoured and privileged
to have Carole Fortune as our guest. Carole is
not only experienced, driven and successful
athlete but also a survivor after a near fatal
road accident almost 7 years ago. Thanks to
Claire Dalrymple for organising dinner"*

I achieved some reasonable Edinburgh Marathon times over the years: -

2006 3hrs 18   2nd AG 40-44 10th F overall

2007 3hrs 24   4th AG

2008 3hrs 26   8th AG 45-49

Loch Ness Marathon was becoming another regular on the calendar offering a great alternative if you want to avoid big-city races. The Loch Ness Marathon route offers extraordinary scenery and splendid isolation apart from fellow runners. It is commonly known that the Baxters Loch Ness Marathon is hilly, but the route is predominantly downhill and many people get a 'PB' on the course. The route, follows a spectacular point-to-point route alongside the world-famous Loch Ness, starting in an atmospheric moorland setting between Fort Augustus and Foyers then continuing through stunning Highland scenery along the south-eastern shores of Loch Ness, across the River Ness, finishing in Inverness, the capital city of the Highlands

We are bussed to the start venue which gives the impression of a hill race rather than a marathon. There are rows of portaloos, a pulsating announcement music system and trucks for baggage. The remote surroundings of moorland, conifer woodland and unrestricted mountain views make you want to reach for your compass and trail running shoes. A bagpipe band, in ceremonial guard of honour, pipe us at the start to set us off. In the beginning the route descends several hundred metres with hardly and spectators only some applause from a few remote residential homes. The tree-lined route provides shade, but through the trees Urquhart Castle can clearly be seen across the loch. There are hills in the first half and later at mile 20 it is a the long slog out from the village of Dores then the steeper hill that follows is energy sapping. Onwards it levels out and remains flat all the way to the finish line.

Loch Ness Marathon times

2006 3:18 2nd Female over 35

2007 3:32 3rd Female over 45

2008 3:23 5th Female over 45

2010 3:42 First marathon post-accident

Certainly, training for and racing marathons places undue amounts of stress on your body, and it is inevitable that our bodies start to break down in the form of constant injuries that keep us just off the best efforts. I start and finish, but it looks very much like my best efforts are over, time off from hard racing and training to mend some of the wear and tear.

I continued around this pace and finishing time for several years running London, Edinburgh Marathons and Loch Ness now becoming a routine until I started to suffer regularity with Achilles Tendonitis. I started to cross train a bit more regularly, introducing swimming and cycling into training to give me a rest from street pounding.

It was time to find a new passion.

2 SURVIVING TRIATHLONS

Having grown a bit weary of training solely for marathons and as I was enjoying the cross training and it was going well, I turned to triathlons to have a try! Never too old to try something new. Swimming, cycling and running, three sports guaranteeing a new challenge, working all the major muscle groups and reducing the injuries I'd accumulated from running alone. It was also less impact on the joints and great for overall fitness and endurance. Regular swimming is also a fantastic zero-impact cardiovascular exercise, what's not to like about it. A decent challenge.

Being a beginner, I started with the Sprint triathlon distance, Swim: 750m,
Bike: 20km and Run: 5km. Three sports in one event so with having done the minimum of training for a race I tackled the Scottish Borders Triathlon Sprint Series, Galashiels, Peebles, Eyemouth, Selkirk, Kelso and Hawick. In my first attempts at this new venture

I placed 2nd Female Vet in Kelso and 6th
Female overall then in Selkirk I was 8th Female
and 3rd Female Vet.

I was always very nervous before the events
kicked off, with swimming being my weakest
discipline, Therefore, I was almost usually in
the first wave to start in the pool. After exiting
the pool and transitioning as quick as
practicable it was onto the bike ride where I
could push it a bit faster being stronger on the
bike than in a pool. The run was my strongest
discipline where it was exhilarating to pass
several people, encouraging me to surge on.

To compete in Triathlons and to start from
scratch, it is an expensive sport and I spent a
vast sum of money just to get to the start line of
a race mainly on an adequate bike. I
understood this before I ventured on, buying
gear to last several years, not skimping on
quality.

I was reveling in these Triathlons looking
forward to the next one gaining improvement
by increasing training to move up to the next
distance to Standard – Olympic triathlon
distance Swim: 1.5km Bike: 40km Run: 10k

The experts say under 3hrs is a really solid time for this distance. At the elite level, Alistair Brownlee famously triumphed at the London Olympics with a time of 1:46:25 at this distance.

How else to ensure you don't drink too much on Hogmanay than to start the year by taking part in the iconic Edinburgh Triathlete's New Year's Day Triathlon. This was a bit tougher than a sprint distance and is a race for everyone, hangovers galore, with a great mix of first-timers looking for a bit fun and also the more seasoned triathlete looking to test their winter training. The swim is 400m (eight lengths of the Royal Commonwealth Pool) where you start at one end of the pool and duck under the rope the next lane and so on until the exit at opposite side. The bike is three laps on roads closed to traffic, done clockwise around Arthur's Seat in Holyrood Park, with 110m of climbing each lap giving a total of 16.53km. The run is once around the same loop as the bike course (again clockwise), a distance of 5.63k. My first year, 2008, overall time was 1hr 23 mins, 10 mins for swim, bike 43 mins and run 29 mins.

Pool Swim Training

Following year, 2009, was an improvement : –
1hr 18, swim 8.13 cycle 40.05 Run 28.04 - 1st
Female Vet and 6th Female overall

Etape Caledonia 2008 – 81-mile cycle.
The Etape Caledonia was the bike challenge to
increase my cycling experience, along with
another thousand riders taking part and cycling
on completely closed roads in the Scottish
Highlands. It is breath-taking and challenging
terrain, the 81-mile (130 kilometres) route
starts in the Perthshire town of Pitlochry and
then heads out into the Highlands around Loch
Rannoch and Loch Tummel. An ex-marine,
friend turned athlete Iain Rankin convinced me

to take part and given the location, guaranteed a hilly route – just under 2,000 metres of climbing. I cycled the course with no hazards where I tested my first experience of drafting – it is allowed in this race, cycling as close as you dare to the cyclist in front shielding from the wind. 2009 Etape Caledonia was a very different story when a church elder was accused of sabotaging the race by scattering thousands of tacks during the race. Several hundred cyclists had their tyres punctured by the tacks. Etape Caledonia is the only cycle race in the UK where all the roads are closed to other traffic during the event, which angered some local people because of the disruption it caused. The race had to be stopped for about an hour-an-a-half after tacks were discovered on parts of the route. The church elder from Pitlochry, was accused of showing a complete disregard for the safety of the participants in the event. The incident received a lot of publicity in the media and forums and the race continues despite the incident.

The race took me 4hrs 54 mins – 81 miles

Corrieyairak Duathlon 2008

After Edinburgh and London marathons and Etape Caledonia it was time to join two disciplines together for a duathlon and so Iain again convinced me to do The Corrieyairak Challenge 2008, a mountain Duathlon. We entered as a team, the Brigadoon Harriers, but it was as an individual, I claimed two awards; Ladies Duathlon 3rd Female and 2nd Vet 40+. The challenge consisted of a 17-mile hill run over the historic Corrieyairack mountain pass (2350ft) followed by a 26-mile bike race. It starts in Garva Bridge, where General Wade's pass crosses the River Spey, and finishes at the village of Kincraig. The route followed in the footsteps of Bonnie Prince Charlie over Scotland's highest mountain road (2526ft). General Wade's historic mountain pass was built by hand in 1731 and successfully defended by Bonnie Prince Charlie in 1745. After the race, we camped in the field overnight after the Ceilidh celebrations.

Lochore Open Water Triathlon 2008

The Bruce Open Water Standard distance at Lochore Meadows Country Park was open water swimming good race training. The swim distance of 1500 metres, in the enclosed nature loch in the park of Lochore. The cycle course was all left turns back to the Loch and the run, entirely within the country park is mostly on paths and is traffic free.

The race took 1hr 28 mins 2nd Female Vet

Moving up to Middle Distance (Half Ironman) the experts advise a good time for this triathlon as the distance is very individual and the course can play a big part. For the 35-39 group, a good men's time is approx. 6 hours and 7 hours for women.

Half-Ironman triathlon distance Swim:1.9km Bike: 90km Run: 21.1km

Aberfeldy Middle Distance championship race 2008. The Baltic waters of Loch Tay is where the swim takes place, just beside Kenmore (6 miles from Aberfeldy). One lap, anti clockwise, across Loch Tay. It was very cold, 13 degrees, considering that it was mid-August. Once you got going and found your rhythm it was actually quite pleasant, due to the calm waters and the security of many canoeists scouting and keeping a close eye out in case anyone got into difficulty.

The cycle 90km (750m climbing). I changed 'quickly' in the transition area to set out and tackle the climb over to Loch Rannoch via the looming, Schiehallion. The course was excellent, roads were quiet and smooth with three well stocked fuel stations. Although there is a bit of a climb that you have to do both ways, the scenery is breath-taking which helped to take your mind off your burning quads knowing that there is still a half marathon to run.

Run - 21km (out and back – rolling). Running shoes on and before I knew it, I was out on the road again passing a few and a few overtaking me, as it was an out and back you see those in front of you as they run towards you and onwards to the finish line. Having distance markers every kilometre and water stations every two, helped break it up. The road itself also had very few cars on and it certainly not flat. Cheered on by the locals in Aberfeldy, you run your way through the town to that all-important finish line and the announcer calls out your name, making you feel like you've just won the Olympics, an exhilarating gesture. A challenging but well organised event, which is set in the magnificent surroundings of Perthshire and much less is charged to enter than an Ironman. The Aberfeldy Tri is an outstanding event even with the midges and freezing waters of Loch Tay. There was enough tenacity in this mountain pass to make it feel like you're taking part in a special event especially when you find out at the awards you have placed 3rd in your Age Group Category in a Championship Event.

3rd Female Vet 5:43:03 mins

Improving in Triathlons and getting results I was interested in how to Qualify for the GB Age-Group team. In order to qualify I had to have a membership to gain a race licence by joining the Home Nation Association – Scottish Triathlon

Then Choose a Championship race you'd like to qualify for. I chose Holten in Austria Olympic distance, then registered paying the £10 registration fee to enable you to register your intent to qualify for the Championship. There are a set of specified qualification races for each Championship event and you are required to qualify via one of these races, a list of which can be found on the British Triathlon Age Group Major Events Calendar.

For these events you are required to submit your best past race performance and supply information regarding your finishing time, the winning time of the athlete in your age-group and also a link to the race result website to complete your submission.

Ampleforth Leg warmer Tri247 2008

Ampleforth was on the list to qualify so I set off with a fellow Triathlete Paul Masterston, who was intending to qualify as well. It was a pool-based sprint distance race from Ampleforth College / Abbey in Scenic Yorkshire Woods surroundings. It was a hilly cycle route on quiet roads finishing with a Cross country run around the Abbey College grounds. The results were displayed on a monitor in a tent in the field, Paul and I waited tentatively to see if we had qualified or not. We both did, securing a place in the ETU in the 2009 Holten ETU Triathlon European Championships 45-49 AG.

Swim 14.09, bike 1:19 run 42.55 3rd F vet.

2009 Knockburn Loch, Banchory, Standard Distance Triathlon and treating this as training for open water swim triathlons. 1500m Open Water Swim. Wetsuits compulsory and a 30-minute cut-off time in reedy shallow water then a 40km Cycle out and back circuit, over undulating, quiet country roads. 10km Run. - hilly undulating route.

2:38:09 1st Female Vet.

70.3 Austria Ironman 24 May 2009 St Polten

My triathlon inspirer and guru, Iain Rankin, convinced me again, to do a full Ironman so in preparation I signed up for Ironman 70.3 (half Ironman) Austria 2009. Iain had previously participated in other Ironmen events and he made me feel confident that I could finish the race with a good time. It seemed like an age away, needless to say the time flew by, interspersed with a few races. Training was going well but as always, the weeks up to the race you naturally have some doubts. Have I done enough training? Holding back on the bike was easy but could I still manage a decent time? Can I manage to run the whole half marathon? But more important, was I going to finish this race and finish in one piece?

Packing a bike is not a lot of fun and I was having to borrow a bike box from my Triathlon Club, Edinburgh Triathletes. After re-checking list upon list, I was on my way to St. Polton, Austria, for the Ironman 70.3 World Championship (the culmination of the Ironman 70.3 series of races that take place during the

12 months prior leading up to the event). There were lots of bikes at the airport all going to the same race. We had hired a car so we could drive to our accommodation where we met many others in for the race.

We were a good bit away from the event so no recce of the race route nor did we go to the pasta party. We registered and collected our numbers, had a look around the expo and then put our bikes in transition and transition bags on their relevant racks and headed back to the hotel. That was it, race preparation was over, now time to get our heads down and mentally prepare for the race.

Alarms were set early, I woke then set about getting some breakfast down my neck, as much as I could stomach and a lot of energy drink was polished off rather quickly before we drove off to the race. I do remember one athlete trying to consume 10 slices of toast! It was about 5:30am and everyone was in transition or milling around tinkering with their bikes, trying to burn off that little bit of nervous energy. My bike was now set for the day, was I?

We headed off to the swim start and before we knew it, the hooter went for us to start so everyone made their way into the water. This is where the "fun" began! It was carnage! There were arms and legs everywhere, everyone trying to find a little bit of space to get into their swim rhythm. I took my fair share of kicks to the ribs and hits round the head from everyone, even though I'd made sure to hang back so I didn't get caught up in the carnage. The swim was in two lakes where you run across a slipway to enter the next one.

I managed to get through T1 (transition 1) with no hassles and I started the bike leg in a positive mood heading to the hilly route and I seemed to be zipping along, the roads were nice and smooth and the general pace was pretty quick. As I am not a great biker, I knew that loads of others would over- take me on the bike I was trying not to let that discourage me, everything was going well, effort was spot on and my average speed was above what I thought it might be. Riding in these hills was fantastic with the support from the locals and others' supporters was amazing, it was a bit like some of the Tour de France climbs when the supporters are literally on top of you shouting and screaming, blowing whistles and clapping, really amazing. The final run in to transition is pretty flat, so it gives you some time to prepare for the run; I took in some final nutrition and started to think about the entry into the Iron Village and the transition area. I get off the bike, my feet were still wet after taking bike shoes off. In the transition area after racking my bike, trainers on and helmet off and ready to go. After a mile or two I started to appreciate how hot it was out there! Even at this stage so many people were surprisingly walking, but yes it was so tough. This is where you really appreciate the awesome support that is out on the course. The finish line came into view just once around the track which was just exhilarating experience, just one of the best feelings in the world so much better than I had thought it would be. I high fived anyone who had their arms outstretched.

Overall, Ironman 70.3 Austria was an amazing race. The people and other triathlon supporters are so friendly, the support from the locals is ace and the scenery is stunning. I was really pleased with my race. After checking the race results, I saw that I was 3rd place Age Group so we stayed on for the presentation that evening. I was awarded with my Ironman Trophy in front of a huge audience and getting up on the stage was more nerve wracking than the race. I was very pleased with the result of my first Ironman Event and the finish time was a real bonus for me.

Ironman Austria 70.3 swim - 39:48 bike - 3:03:16 run - 1:42:44. Total 5:31:20

3rd Female Vet securing me a beautiful glass 'M dot' Trophy

On stage receiving Ironman Trophy

2009 Holten ETU Triathlon European Championships

The Championship Event had arrived during a European wide heatwave in the lead up to the race where we saw temperatures rise into the high 30s, with an inevitable knock on effect to triathlon with St Holten being declared a non-wetsuit swim. It was announced early on and confirmed that the water was more like a bath than a lake. The confirmation of a non-wetsuit swim in the race briefing prompted silence and provided the first take home bit of advice: practice open water swimming without a wetsuit. Many competitors were mentally unprepared for this despite the higher temperatures being experienced. The lack of wetsuit will make most swimmers slower, but it is the same for everyone and is essentially the same as every other pool swim that has been completed in preparation. In fact, the higher water temperature would have made for a very uncomfortable swim and a real risk of overheating if they had of been worn.

The swim course was not one of the best that I have completed but with clear blue water it was beautiful scenery. We had to dive in, needless to say I had never dived in anywhere wearing goggles therefore, I spent a lot of time rehearsing the start. The swim heads out, across the lake, and exits up a jetty towards the transition area which was lined with spectators and supporters cheering you on towards transition.

Into transition 1 and the run into the bikes meant that there was no time for hanging around with the other competitors. The day before it is vital to orientate yourself and locate your racking position in the sea of bikes. Thankfully, I had a good straightforward racking position, I found my bike quickly and set off.

The scenery on the bike course was spectacular, it did its job and distracted you from the tough climbs - you certainly had to have your wits about you on the fast descents. The real focus here was to combat the high temperatures by ensuring I was adequately hydrated and taking on sufficient nutrition. All was going to plan to ensure I did the best I could with fast descents back towards Transition 2.

Into T2 and on to the run as quickly as I could, I was feeling quite strong as I had stuck to refueling strategies during the race. The high temperatures earlier in the day had created real difficulties in hydrating myself but I powered through. The run course had an unbelievable finish where you could picture the Brownlee brothers racing alongside you. We had met them in the athlete's village and had a short chat with them, always inspiring. The run becomes a bit of a mental battle, where your mind always tries to tell your body that you are more tired than you are. To combat this, I broke the course down into smaller sections to keep focused.

What a buzz I got when I saw James Cracknell at the finish line, knowing I had raced on the same course as him.

C Fortune 7th 45-49 Age Group GBR

Swim: 30:24 Cycle: 1:14 Run: 47:59 Total: 2:32:25

All geared up for Triatlon Holten 2009

IRONMAN UK – Bolton – Aug 2nd 2009

Full Ironman triathlon distance - Swim: 3.8km
Bike:180km Run: 42.2km

What's a good time for this triathlon distance? "Just completing the distance within the 17hr cut-off is a massive accomplishment! But anything around the 13hrs mark for men (30-35) is a solid time; 14hrs for women. Getting under the 11hr mark deserves serious respect!"

This was my first, and unfortunately last, Ironman, I had enjoyed the build-up/journey to this event immensely. I drove down to the event with my bike on the back of the car the day before and checked into a hotel for two nights. It had been torrential rain in the preceding days and I had wished I had brought my welly boots for registration/transition area as cars were being pulled out of the mud by a local farmer and his tractor, other cars were left abandoned in anger. Ironically, this area was also the camping platform for many of the athletes and their poor families, knee deep in mud and pouring rain.

Saturday (day before race day) – registration and bike check in with the chance to look at the swim in the reservoir to get a feel of the water and get your bearings. I'd heard it was 12c and I knew that was pretty cold so I didn't want to prove it by getting my wetsuit wet and cold for the 6am start the next morning. One thing that did become apparent was that the route from the reservoir to the bike transition area had a gradient greater than 14% which was one thing I wasn't looking forward to.

I racked the bike. I never bothered to recce the

cycle route or the run route, take what you get.

Race day started at the hotel from 3.15am, with breakfast. My friend Julie, who I had met in Austria 70.3, and I arrived at the reservoir to a distinct buzz of nervous athletes who were checking tyre pressures, loading up bikes with nutrition and climbing into their wetsuits.

It was cold and I couldn't wait to get into the 12c water! We were herded through a gate and then descended down the steep narrow lane to the reservoir where some swimmers must've been treading water for at least 15minutes until all 1500 competitors finally got into the water.

There was some confusion as the overzealous DJ was telling us to move back behind the start line, just as the claxon sounded. We were off with a loud round of "Uggy, uggy, uggy, oi oi oi" in deep water and the battle began, getting kicked in the face and stomach whilst trying not to drown. This took the mind off the water temperature. I thought the crowds of swimmers would thin out due to the various swimming abilities but it seemed to take at least 1000m before this was the case.

Exiting the reservoir, I staggered left and right, up and down, it seemed the cold in my ears had affected my balance but luckily there were some young men positioned as 'catchers' who physically pointed me in the direction of the steep climb to the transition as they are not allowed to help you. T1 had been refurbished with straw and a red carpet to cover the ankle-deep mud, although, you could still feel the squelch as you ran over it. T1 took time taking off the wetsuit, and slipping into a cycling top whilst trying to thaw out a little before embarking on the bike.

Bike – 3 laps of 38 (ish) miles

Bearing in mind it was still only 07:30, there was a distinct nip in the air, although we knew the sun was on its way. I was worried I had not worn enough clothes but the first climb was underway and the heart began pumping hard. I was not enjoying the cycle very much and to be honest I could not wait to get off the bike but I did manage to overtake some people. The steep ascent of the 3rd lap caused trouble and I thought I was about to 'bonk'. I had some fuel and carried on with the cycle and somehow reached transition 2, reverting to a relieved smile and ready to tackle the final part of the course - the marathon.

Run – out – back – out (finishing at the town hall)

Out of transition I felt great, I smiled and waved at the people gathering. The beginning of the run leg seemed to pass quickly and the streets were lined with amazingly friendly crowds, the sun was hot and my motivation and confidence was growing as this mission was within grasp. The 1st turnaround point seemed to take forever and I didn't know the exact mileage. The terrain was undulating in the park and I drank as I ran past the water stops. I could tell by the noise of the crowd that I was almost at the finish line. All sorts of emotion and excitement passed, I saw this amazing big screen at the end of a red carpet with a clock in front which said 12hrs 35min – I couldn't believe it! I thought it would take me over 13hrs. I saw my friend Maire and her daughter who was obviously expecting me to be collapsing on my knees. I was elated and grinned from ear to ear but I had my eye on the clock so I sprinted to the finish in order to secure a time of 12hrs 35 mins. The DJ announced "Your 2nd in your class and you're an IRONMAN".

Of all race finishes this has to be the most emotional moving finish I have ever experienced. I was presented with my second M Dot Trophy on a stage with the lady who won first place, she took the Iconic Kona, the Ironman World Championship place that was up for grabs, if she had refused it, it is rolled down to the next person.

As I had drove down to Bolton for the race myself, I was dreading the drive home as my body was sore and tired from the race. That was when my good friend Bill very kindly offered to take the train down and drive me home, in which I did not hesitate to reply "yes please".

Swim: 1:22:15 Cycle: 6:44:19 Run 4:10:42

Total 12:35:33 ~2nd Female Vet

Bolton Ironman UK Trophy 2nd F 45-49 2009

August 15th 2009, I swam the leg of the
Aberfedly Middle Distance Triathlon in a team
for my club, Edinburgh Triathletes, with Fiona
Zeiner on the run and Andrew McMenigall on
the bike. Andrew and his friend were very sadly
killed by a lorry driver in 2011, they were only
40 miles into LEJOG, the 960mile route from
Lands' End to John o' Groats. The driver was
jailed for 8 years for dangerous driving.

The next adventure was a cycle trip from
Edinburgh to Paris. (Unfortunately I did not do)

August 16th 2009.

I set off on a bike ride from home on a circular loop in the countryside. I left my daughter Jade to look after her younger brother, Ryan. The lady up the road waved and said 'be careful'. None of this I can remember and I only know from others what happened that fateful day. My last recollection is driving home from the Aberfeldy race the day before.

The driver had been performing in the Edinburgh Festival and was on his way home driving his Jaguar along the country road I was cycling on. He hit me at 50 miles an hour, the impact threw me onto the car's windscreen which my body smashed as I went through it. I was then carted down the road on the bonnet before being thrown off at the other side of the road.

The impact to my head resulted in my skull being fractured, giving me an 'acquired brain injury', my neck was broken in two places, I had various cuts to my forehead, eye and cheeks, my legs were cut but not broken.

A runner, Chris Burns, now a good friend, was driving past at the time and stopped to help as he could see I was in a bad way, apparently, I was trying to stand up but my neck was at an odd angle. Fortunately, a passenger in another vehicle was medically trained, the director of the NHS, at the time, stopped to assist. They called an ambulance and I was taken to the Royal Infirmary to be stabilised. The neck break was the main concern and an MRI scan was conducted which revealed I would need surgery to have a metal plate inserted on two vertebrae, Cervical 5 and Cervical 6, to provide stability. C5 and C6 provide flexibility and support to your neck and the nerve supply to neck, arms, hands and shoulders. I was extremely lucky not to be paralysed in these areas. The operation was carried out in the Western General hospital, where I remained, for two weeks. Once I was stable enough again, I was moved to Astley Ainslie Hospital due to the acquired brain injury. The hospital is for long-stay patients who have suffered brain injuries, mental health issues along with other conditions.

Daily I underwent a memory test, physiotherapist tests with exercises then tests with the Occupational Therapist and tests with the psychiatrist. The ward in the evening could be very noisy with patients having sleep terrors (night terrors), it was in my best interest to be released as soon as possible. I soon learned to say everything was just perfect to the Dr when he was on his daily visits and also to the ward nurses. I finally got out on a weekend trial at home to make sure I would be okay to live on my own at home, I passed the test and was released after a six week stay.

I had a surgical collar on my neck to keep me upright, for the duration of nine weeks to stop me turning my neck left and right and to assist the plate to fuse to the bone in the correct locations. After having another MRI scan, to make sure the bones had knitted together properly, I received a phone call at home advising me that I could remove the collar, naturally I was apprehensive about removing the collar thinking that my head would fall off!

After getting out of hospital, I was determined to start walking as soon as I could, as I didn't want the injury to stop me. Within a few weeks of the collar coming off I started to go out for a walk gradually introducing bursts of jogging.

The surgeon advised me not to take up cycling again, the fixed vertebrae in my neck give limited mobility making looking left and right difficult. I have never been back on a bike since.

The driver was never charged, even although he was driving too close to me, claiming I had pulled out in front of him! Only he knows the truth in that statement. He had been performing in the Edinburgh festival on the Saturday evening and driving home on the quiet route to England. I did try to pursue what had happened but it was getting too complicated and I was not in any fit state of mind or health to deal with it and just wanted to recover and not dwell on it. We all know the new legislation changes in the distance to pass a cyclist as many motorists had been ignoring the recommended distance of 1.5 metres.

Cyclists are far more likely to be killed or injured on the road than other road users. I was very fortunate that I was in a strong state of health at the time of the accident which helped me to recover immensely.

Iain had lent me his top end Mavic road wheels (performance wheels with low drag for speed) for the Ironman UK, the wheels were still on the bike when I was hit by the car, although the bike was a write off the wheels survived with minimum damage.

It was time to find a new passion.

The Daily Record Article

3 ULTRAMARATHON RUNNING

March 2012 was my first attempt at an Ultramarathon race, where else to start? something just a bit longer than a marathon and flat as well. The D33 runs from Aberdeen's Duthie park to Banchory and back using mostly a disused railway line. This makes the route straightforward with little ascent/descent to deal with but also it is not the most exciting route. The D33 is more like a road marathon with a bit added on with the main benefit being it was not on tarmac. During the race I managed to hold a reasonable pace for the first half but I slowed down a bit in the later miles. I was in training for the London Marathon so it was a good race to get the mileage in your legs. Reaching the turnaround point in good spirits where my drop bag was, I found it, selected what I needed and headed back. I passed the three-quarter way checkpoint still reasonably comfortable, could I manage sub five hours? My pace did slow down considerably not having run this distance before but these twenty miles plus runs were paying off. I pushed on knowing the finish was not too far away, last few miles less than two miles to go enjoying the thought of finishing my first Ultra in a reasonable time. I saw the entry gate to Duthie park and I was relieved to see a sign that meant only a few 100 metres to run.

I crossed the finish line rather delighted in finishing in one piece in 5 hours and 4 mins, enjoyed it and knew I would be back for more Ultra marathons.

The D33 is really well organised and a great event if you want to find a way of going beyond marathon distance. I actually went back to do the D33 in 2013, managing to get my sub 5 hours this time - 4:58! and also again in 2014 finishing in exactly the same time 4:58 as 2013, consistent! Both times securing me an Age Group Trophy.

Receiving my award for the D33 from George Reid, Race Director

Goodies from the D33

As I had enjoyed the challenge of the D33 so much I decided to take part in the Glen Ogle 33 Ultra later that year. I had heard it was difficult to get a place in this small race. When the entries opened, I jumped at the chance to have a stab at my second Ultra. The GO33 is just up the road as such! I gave a lift to two 'pro' ultra-runners, Karl & Caroline who had run the Jedburgh three peaks the weekend before and who gave great inspiring stories to listen to on the journey up. On the start line of the race I found my friend Claire Dalrymple, not knowing that she was running it, great to see another friendly face.

In 2015 the race started from Killin and not Strathyre, due to a flood at the campsite used for parking and the pre-race set up. This meant BaM racing had to make some last-minute changes. The main change for the runners was the reversal of the traditional route, with a few changes. In the first half, now the new route, it was flat but then gave way to a tough few miles of climbing out of Killin following cycle route 7. There were three major climbs on the route with a section on the road and a trail down over the viaduct towards Balquhidder. It was strange running over the shoogly bridge and into the old finish line knowing you still had another 15 or so miles to run. From this point it is down the hill towards the Checkpoint at Balquhidder and back onto the cycle path with it eventually getting steeper to the turnback point at Lochearnhead. Heading to the finish it is a nice downhill into Killin but there is a cruel loop around the park to the finish line. This was the route I run in 2015 after nursing an injury with not a lot of training. As the race places are non-transferable, I decided to attempt it! It took me a bit longer time to finish this year, 5hrs 48 mins and in 2012 (5hrs 23 mins when it started in Strathyre) and around 1km longer! Excuses!

In 2012 I was nominated to carry the Olympic Torch by the local community who recognised my recovery and determination to get back into running after the accident. I was nominated in the inspirational category and made it through the selection process, passed background and security checks and "had my moment to shine" as a Torchbearer carrying the Olympic Flame. The search was across the UK looking for extraordinary people who have a burning passion and use it to spread happiness and inspire others; "these are our future flames and you are one of them" it said on the email confirming my selection that I was part of the London 2012 team.

It was on Wednesday 13th June 2012 in Falkirk and what an experience it was. The Torchbearers all met at the Falkirk Wheel where we were put on a bus and driven to our allocated section. When you arrived, you were dropped off to meet with the previous torchbearer who was to pass the flame onto your torch, it was your turn to carry the flame for that brief mile with the police escorts behind and in front of you, onwards towards the next torchbearer to repeat the process. The streets were lined with people cheering and waving enthusiastically and in particular around the schools which were lined with hundreds of pupils. Just in front of the torch process was the Coca Cola bus which was blasting an outstanding presentation adding to the hype. When you had finished your stretch, you jumped back on the bus with the other torchbearers again all exchanging exciting stories to be driven back to the Falkirk Wheel. I wore the tracksuit that we had all been issued with for the rest of the day. Wearing it that evening I ventured into Edinburgh City to watch the procession ending for the day at Edinburgh City Castle. Emilie Sande was playing the closing ceremony to Edinburgh on the stage to a huge audience.

Jade, Ryan and myself with Olympic Torch 2012

Passing the flame to a fellow Torch bearer

The Lochalsh Dirty 30 has to be my favourite
Ultra race, we basked in wall to wall
sunshine, that weekend in 2013. Memories of
sea Lochs, overlooking Skye surrounded by
magnificent mountains and to top it an
outstanding house for the weekend in a prime
location at the entrance to Glenelg. The
adventure started on Friday evening with a
trip up with friends Claire and Alan, who
drove us there, unfortunately with a route
diversion via Loch Lomond due to an accident
taking over 5 hours to get from Callander to
Glenelg.

On the morning of the race there was low cloud
clinging to mountains around and on Skye, it
wasn't cold, and the forecast was for sunshine
later. After breakfast and accumulating our
gear together we headed down to registration
at the Glenelg community hall. There was
almost two hundred walkers and runners taking
part giving an impressive atmosphere when we
arrived. We registered with ease and joined the
gaggle outside for the briefing. The race
started with last years' winner Scot Kennedy

and ultra-runner Donnie Campbell leading the way with only approximately over 30 runners and over 140 walkers.

The route starts on narrow roads leading towards the Glenelg/Skye Ferry point with the sunshine starting to break through. The first incline is just before the Ferry point up a path that traverses a coastal ridge. We pass the first check point and continue to the next section Ardintoul to Letterfearn, where we follow a road briefly inland and steeply uphill, I could see other runners were already at the top, some heading left along the 30-mile route, where Alan very kindly waited on Claire and I making sure we took the correct path. Others were on the shorter route heading back inland to complete the 12-mile route.

Onto a woodland where the path mostly disappears and reappears as you follow fire breaks in the forest. Event organizers had put out the usual red and white streamers on the route making the route easy to follow, and thanks to the recent dry weather the wooded section was only a little muddy in places - it's this section that gives the Dirty 30 its name but not this year, I was pleased to experience.

The forest opened out to a spectacular view with the Skye Bridge reaching out gracefully over the water in the distance towards the West with the first glimpses of Eilean Donan Castle across the shore.

On the Lettterfearn to Shiel Bridge section I spotted a table laid out with jelly babies and water, what a welcoming sight. Then at Rattagan the youth hostel had put out a table beside the road with cups and jug of water very much appreciated on a hot day. Shiel Bridge was a relief to see, the half way point and I was pleased to see I hadn't gotten lost!

A narrow path rises uphill on a mountain which I walked up knowing I still had over ten miles to go. After descending the route continues across rough moorland which is mostly runnable with a small river crossing into a forest track that has been felled leading into Moyle. At the checkpoint there is more water before heading to Balvraid. I had expected the finish to be closer as we approached Glenelg, I managed to find some energy with the thought of securing a time of under 6 hours but only just missed it. I finished in 6:01 and Donnie Campbell came in first setting a new course record 4:15

We had a lovely evening in our garden with champagne sharing our stories and thankful of great weather and a great event.

Campbell, Donnie	4 hours 15 minutes
Gallie, David	5 hours 22 minutes
Lyons, Karen	5 hours 22 minutes
Harrington, Patrick	5 hours 35 minutes
Osfield, Robert	5 hours 37 minutes
Lees, George	5 hours 39 minutes
Leggett, Mark	5 hours 41 minutes
Leggett, Helen	5 hours 43 minutes
Clements, Gordon	5 hours 44 minutes
Morrison, Gary	5 hours 53 minutes
Britain, Frances	5 hours 59 minutes
Redgrove, James	6 hours 0 minutes
Fortune, Carole	6 hours 1 minutes
Owen, Russell	6 hours 3 minutes
Vinall, Jo	6 hours 7 minutes

from the Moray Firth to the finish line at Cluny
Square in Buckie I managed to get myself lost
– I imagined I saw marshals at the top of the
road and I ran up towards them. The marshals
turned out to be dog walkers! I scouted around
and saw a bridge that I ran to where I could
see the runners below me and shouted to ask
how I could get back on the track, my detour
had added on approximately 1 mile. The road I
was on and the track finally merged together
and I headed up the hill to the finish to be told I
was 1st FV and won a wonderful bottle of
Benromach Scotch Whisky. I really enjoyed the
race and the course has a gentle beauty to it
with a mixture of trails and the beach.

The West Highland Way Race was in the back
of my mind and as I was gaining lots of
experience in Ultra running so I just had to
have a bash at it. Not only is it one of the
world's longest established ultra-marathons,
it's almost 100 miles, 95 to be exact. The
WHW is run along the trail between Milngavie
(just north of Glasgow) to Fort William in the
Scottish Highlands, ninety-five miles through
four counties, 14,000 feet of climb and a 35-
hour cut off time. After all, I had ran the second

half of it in 2014, the Devil O' the Highlands and thoroughly enjoyed it.

I was picked up at 9pm in the evening of the race as registration takes place on the evening of the race between 9.00pm and midnight at St Joseph's RC Church Hall in Milngavie and the race starts at Milngavie Station 1:00am. At registration I collected my race number, my goody bag and purchased merchandise. One member of your support crew attends registration and is given a support crew permit which needs to be displayed on the support vehicle for the full race. Everyone is weighed and given a weighing card, to be produced later at the weigh-in stations at Auchtertyre, Kinlochleven and Fort William.

We are given a short race briefing near the start line at 12.30am and we start at exactly 1.00am at the start of the West Highland Way, at the bridge beside Milngavie station.

We have to check in at a number of checkpoints throughout the race. The checkpoints have strict cut-off times.

- Balmaha (19miles) – 5hrs 0 mins
- Beinglass Farm (42miles) – 12hrs 0 mins
- Auchtertyre (51miles) – 15hrs 30 mins
- Bridge of Orchy (60miles) – 18hrs 30 mins

- Glencoe Ski Centre (71miles) – 23hrs 0 mins
- Kinlochleven (81miles) – 28hrs 0 mins
- Fort William (95miles) – 35hrs 0 mins

Chris Burns was my support crew for the first section at Drymen who brought me my food and cheered on, I was very strict with instructions that I do not like to stop so bring what I want to me and run with me and take any rubbish from me. If I stop, I find it difficult to start again, especially in latter stages when sore. On Conic Hill, it is day light, head torch off and a nice walk up the hill and down into Balmaha to meet the support crew again.

First weigh in at Auchtertyre, I was inquisitive and remarked "hopefully lost a bit weight as going my holidays the next day". This comment did not go down very well! Yes, I know it is serious but I was just having bit of light hearted fun. There is no food or water provided at checkpoints; it all needs to be carried by your support crew that follow you in the race in a vehicle for the full event.

The run up towards Jelly baby hill where race devotee Murdo McEwan handed out jelly babies wearing a wonderful colourful outfit.

Up until Auchtertyre one crew member is allowed then from Auchtertyre onwards you need a crew of at least two people, one of whom has the pleasure of 'running' the last two stages with you. Erni met me on the section from Auchtertyre Farm and ran with me to Glencoe, I was starting to 'bonk' at this time so she managed to phone down to Craig who was waiting in Glencoe and ask him to bring flat coke to me, it did the trick. Craig ran with me up and over the Devil's staircase to the relentless drop down to Kinlochleven where Erni took over duties again to the finish at Fort William. Poor Erni had a lot to put up with as I rambled on a load of nonsense. The bonfire at Lundavra had been extinguished by the rain and my headtorch battery had died, we were running with one hoping for the daylight to arrive. Eventually it did and we headed along the trail to Glen Nevis road and to the finish.

Faster runners are not allowed to have a support runner at any point during the race, obviously I do not come into this category and no-one is allowed a support runner before Auchtertyre farm.

The section between the top of Loch Lomond and Crianlarich is the most technical, having to avoid tree roots, large pot holes and just general treacherous trails.

The electronic timing is a fantastic implement and each runner is issued with a SPORTident Timing Card (SI-Card) at registration which we

scan at each of the checkpoints points and at
Rowardennan and Lundavra we are
responsible to 'dib' by laying the SI-Card flat
over the hole in the SPORTident Timing station
so the station will beep or flash to indicate that
a timestamp has been recorded on your card.
This gives family and friends the opportunity to
follow your progress throughout the race. At
the finish I was given a small printout showing
my split times through each checkpoint on the
route.

The WHW is a very tough challenge and you
have to read up on and be aware of, the
medical advice on the race website and in
particular they advise not to take Ibuprofen or
other NSAIDs, such as naproxen or diclofenac.
These can cause serious medical problems
during endurance events, any runner taking
Ibuprofen or other NSAIDs may be
disqualified.

Of course, there is mandatory kit such as
lightweight space blanket, a mobile phone with
race emergency numbers programmed in to it,
head torch, with spare batteries, full body
waterproof clothing and a whistle.

The race finish is outside the Nevis Centre in
Fort William, where I was weighed again and
driven by Chris to my hotel room – smelly

shoes at the door which went straight into the bin after a well-deserved bath after 28 hours and 3 mins.

The prizegiving was in the Nevis Centre in Fort William at 12 noon on the next day, the cut off time, where every finisher is presented with their hard-earned goblet. When we travelled back to Edinburgh where my crew stopped off for a coffee whilst I sat in the car unable to move and exhausted to say the least. A family holiday to Majorca was the recovery process and I always recount being in the sea and how the waves lifted my toenails up and down with the tide as they were only attached at the cuticle!

West Highland Way 28hrs 03 seconds

I finished the West Highland Way 95 miles

Hadrian's Wall or the race known as "The Wall" hosted by Rat Race was one of those events I'd had my eye on for a while and after running the West Highland Way I thought it's almost 30 miles shorter, of course I can do it. Running buddy David Nightingale really wanted to do it as well so I was convinced but as with all Rat Race events, it's not a cheap entrance fee. It did look brilliant as it's a great route, well stocked, well supported and just over the border. We entered early and got the cheaper early bird places, which was still not exactly modest at £175, at least less than the full price of over £200

The route of The Wall runs for 69 miles from Carlisle to Newcastle not quite coast to coast, but across the border follows the route of Hadrian's Wall at some points and the course is about 80% road with a few trail sections which are indeed near to sections of the wall. The entire route does not follow the wall completely! There is some climbing and the elevation is only about 1,100 metres.

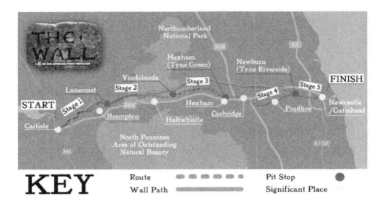

Rat Race Adventure Sports Map for The wall

Registration takes place the day before the race, so we travelled to Carlisle by train staying in a hotel in the centre of town. The race starts at Carlisle Castle where they provide a facility to have a bag sent from the start to the finish, which we used to transport overnight bags to the end. The weather was dry and clear, but not sunny. We had been given a tracker to which was great as a safety feature and excellent for supporters to follow your progress. After the race briefing, we set off at 7:00am, from the square inside the castle grounds, over the drawbridge and out through the park. It was quite congested at first, but soon spread out over the first ten miles which was pretty flat, with just a couple of slight inclines, so a good warm-up at a reasonable pace.

There are two kinds of aid stations along the race route. Five of these are 'Pit Stops', which are stocked with various kinds of food and drink and also six checkpoints, which just have water and sweets. Two of the Pit Stops in the second half were about 18 miles apart but there was plenty food and water to take with you if you wanted to. The first Pit Stop (15 miles) was like a breakfast buffet. The checkpoints all had little bags of sweets such as Skittles and Haribo, which were really easy to grab and pocket. I try not to spend too much time at checkpoints, as it can add up considerably over a long race, but it's important to refuel, and there was an excellent variety of food on offer at all of the Pits Stops, including a range of sandwiches.

At around ten miles there was a sign saying 'That was the easy bit' then we ran into the hilly section in the middle section of the race. The elevation in this event wouldn't really trouble anyone who's used to running on hills, it's more the distance that's the challenge. The route is mostly road and tarmac is much harder on the legs than soft trail. Courses that have gentle inclines rather than steep hills are harder in a way, because you're more tempted to run them, not knowing you're on a hill and just think you are struggling, whereas you'd walk up a steeper gradient. There is some spectacular scenery to enjoy on the route, with Rat Race photographers snapping away.

The main drop bag Pit Stop is at Hexham, 44 miles in. We never needed anything as the race was well organised so we plodded on. Inside the marquee we could see people sitting on chairs and the grass, some sorting out their feet and trying to decide what to eat, what to wear and others clearly trying to decide whether to call it a day but I know the longer you sit down the harder it is to get going again!

Runners had now become quite spread out, but the route is so well marked there was never any danger of getting lost. We ran through some pretty villages and there always seemed to be some people out to give a cheer. We weren't aiming for any particular time just to finish comfortably and to keep moving was the goal! It takes a lot of mental effort to keep pushing on, helping each other in bad moments but we managed to keep running (slowly) on the flat and downhill sections. We started to pass quite a few runners on the way to the final Pit Stop at Newburn, which is 62 miles in. The final stretch was all tarmac, we were both fatigued but excited to see the River Tyne leading into Newcastle proving the finish wasn't far away. Running into the city along the Quayside was great, lots of people seemed to know what was going on and cheered us on as we turned to cross the Millennium Bridge. Just as we reached the finish line, the bridge lifted to let a boat under, we just missed that – Phew. We finished in just under 15 hours 14hrs 51 mins and we both won first place in our age groups, securing us the 1st Joint Runners trophy – a huge slab of 'Hadrian's Wall slate'. We were more than delighted.

There was hot food and showers at the end, but I really wasn't up to eating curry or chilli at that point. David's brother in-law was there to drive us to his house, a very kind and welcoming gesture after 69 miles. The race medal was great and so was the Slate Trophy.

I'd really recommend The Wall, even though it's not cheap. It excels itself in the way it is organised and supported. They really look after you and overall, it's a great event!

The Wall Trophy for First Mixed Pair 2016

SUMS – Scottish Ultra Marathon Series. The Scottish Ultra Marathon Series has certain races which give you points for each event. The best three finishes counting towards the end of season prizes for long series, short series & both series. It was the short series that I won 1st Place Age Group in 2013. In 2014 I won 3rd Place and in 2015 I won 3rd Place Age Group which was awarded in Edinburgh. I never managed to get a 2nd place to complete my whisky decanter and glass set!

I received a lovely email informing me 'Huge congratulations on a fab year of running. You may or may not be aware that your performances in the Scottish Ultra Marathon Series races have cumulated in you winning an award'

The Decanter issued to winners of SUMS 2013

4 HILL RACING AND MUNRO BAGGING

Ultra-running was making me fatter and slower, it was time to find a new passion. I 'retired' to Marathon distance maximum!

Running in the hills saturated by shapes, smells and colours, the sun bursting out revealing breath-taking scenes, green landscape, undulating ridges untouched by civilisation or industry. A long day in the hills to escape from consumerism is satisfaction and then to sit on the grass gazing up reflecting on being part of that race or that run. No material rewards, only £10 to enter and racing for the love of it. I started ticking off the races in the Scottish hill races calendar, 27 to date and 34 Munros, some experiences are well worth a mention.

I started to have an interest in Munro 'bagging' which is Scottish mountains over 3,000ft (914.4 m). They are named after Sir Hugh Munro. A good friend of mine, Alison Barclay, took me to bag my first Munro in April 2013. Climbing these peaks is a great way to explore some of Scotland's best scenery and locations. The highest Munro is Ben Nevis at 4,411ft (1,345 m), although there are many lower and also more challenging Munros to climb, such as the 12 rocky airy peaks of the Black Cuillin on Skye and the UK mainland's narrowest ridge walk - the Aonach Eagach - in Glen Coe.

There are in total 282 Munros and although I started this imaginative ambition, knowing realistically that I will not complete them all and become a 'compleatist' (or Munroist). I added this popular pastime to my new interest of hill racing with the intent to 'run' as many as I can. I am currently standing at only 34 Munros and with the lockdown in place I have not been able to get out so far this year.

August 2016. The South Glen Shiel Ridge is a superb ridge walk where so many peaks can be climbed in a day, with minimal descent between the summits. The views are excellent all the way on this traverse and you bag 7 Munros on well-constructed stalkers' paths. As it is a linear route, we started at Cluanie Inn, Glenmoriston, at the Eastern end of the ridge leaving one car there and drove 11km to park a second car at the finishing site, to enable transport back to the starting point. I set off with a group of walkers and it was obvious by the first Munro we were all different fitness levels and I was approximately 20 mins ahead at each summit, of the group. It was a glorious sunny clear day where you could see for miles. I shadowed the footsteps of another rambler, who I had a confab with about his destination, along the ridge as it stretched out in front of me, always keeping my group in sight. Once on the ridge the way is open and easy to navigate, and the views are extensive, on a good day. The ridge curves slightly to the South before heading towards the impressive Aonach air Chrith. It is a fantastic mountain, the standout of the ridge, one of those peaks you look back on to appreciate where you have walked with its airy summit and sharp ridge cuts. Loch Quoich can be seen looking down to the South and to the North are the Five Sisters. When we reached the final summit, I watched the rambler descend down onto the road below. I waited on my group and then let them continue the walk following their guide book and the walk leader. I however, followed the other rambler to the road, once there I observed the car to take us back to the Cluanie Inn, however as there was no sign of my group, I spotted a Police convoy escorting a wind turbine, I hitched a lift, spoke nicely to the Officer and he very sympathetically gave me a lift to the Clunaie Inn. I phoned my group and informed them where I was asking them what they would like to eat as the restaurant was due to close within the hour. Alas they were not amused as I had split up the walking group, they arrived at the Inn over an hour later to a closed restaurant where I had enjoyed a delicious meal.

On the Glenshiel Ridge

September 2017. Ben Nevis Hill Race 14km 1,340 metres (4409ft). In 1895,William Swan, a

Fort William tobacconist, completed the first recorded timed ascent and descent of Britain's tallest mountain and he could not have envisaged the modern day Ben Nevis Race having a field of 600 runners accepting a challenge which is not for the unfit or faint-hearted . It is very difficult to get a place once you have confirmed your qualification as an experienced Hill Runner to apply. It was 1951 that the Ben Nevis Race Association was founded with the intention of formalising arrangements for an annual race. The first field was twenty-one runners, the race has now grown beyond all recognition and has taken place every year since with the exception of 1980 as the elements won that year. A last-minute decision being made to cancel the race for the safety of the runners and the officials on the mountain. There has, sadly, been one death in the race, as far back as 1957, John Rix of Surrey, who was found sheltering behind a boulder halfway down, slightly off course and shoes lost, he died when being stretchered off the mountain. Severe weather can induce hypothermia, disorientation and exposure, this is the risk you take when you participate in fell races. 1955 was the first-year women were allowed in the Ben Race. 'Lady Runners' classed as a tough race, being the most iconic in Scotland and a supreme test of fitness.

There are time allowances set, the first is halfway in one hour or be turned back, then you must reach the summit in two hours and complete the course in 3 hours 15 minutes or you may be refused entry to subsequent races. The record times for both men and women have stood since 1984 when Kenny Stuart and Pauline Stuart respectively recorded 1h 25m 34s and 1h 43m 01s. Findlay Wild, a GP from Inverness, ran 1 hr 32 in 2019, is the master of Ben Nevis by winning it 10 years in a row.

The race fills up quickly and there are strict entry requirements, providing evidence of completing some category A fell races or mountain marathons. Running buddy, Gala Harriers, David Nightingale, convinced me to enter and we both successfully secured a place, his wife, Anne accompanied us on the journey north to support. There is of course, the standard hill running equipment you must carry; full waterproof body cover including a head covering, gloves, a whistle, map and compass and know how to use both! At registration competitors are issued with a card as confirmation of entry which is handed over at race start additionally, a numbered wristband to be handed in at the summit. The runners are marched around the Shinty pitch behind the piper before handing in our runners cards and lining up at the start line. Then the gun goes and we run towards the edge of the pitch and out on to the road that leads to the Nevis Inn. After a short section of road, we begin the climb towards Ben Nevis. The path becomes increasingly steep and more challenging the higher up you climb with sections where the stones are quite loose and some clambering is involved in various places. Hill runners are renowned for supporting each other which is one of the things I love about hill racing, there is such a feeling that we are all in it together offering words of encouragement. Ascending I can see the lead pack hurling down towards me at a blistering pace, all cautions gone with the wind over treacherous surfaces, skimming over rocks, sending them flying, all choosing slightly different routes through the boulders. I make it up to the Halfway Lochan within the time limit and then to the summit within the two-hour limit, the path flattens a little where the runners turn back over the skyline to start the descent. Then I began the return journey. What I had witnessed with them plummeting recklessly down, I may be paranoid but it appeared too threatening to me, why tempt breaking your neck twice in a lifetime. I opted to take the tourist route down the zig zag path down the middle section adding distance and time. Finally, the paths merge again with the runners, about this point I'm finding this rocky terrain very challenging, then streams of runners seemed to be flying past me and I just told myself to run my own race to get to the finish in one piece. I spent most of the downhill with my eyes firmly focussed two feet in front of me with the odd glance up to make sure I was heading in the right direction. Once on the grassy section I slipped and slid my way down to the stream. Then it was back on to the stone path with huge wide steps leading to the last section on road. I had been looking forward to running on the road again as I wouldn't have to concentrate so hard on where to place my feet. Nearer to the pitch where we started, I could hear the sounds of runners names being called and I had the fulfilment that I was actually going to finish, and within the cut-off time. What a feeling, absolute heaven. David got down before me, proudly displaying two grazed knees after taking a tumble, I'm sure he wasn't the only one. It is a great race to experience, with climbing to the top being the easy bit however, most definitely a one off race for me anyway!

Sep 2017. The Two Breweries Hill Race, Traquair to Broughton, 30km, 1500ft. The bus leaves Broughton for Traquhair at 10am, with race registration at Traquhair. Undoubtedly, there is strict kit-checks before the race and we are counted through. Finally, the gun sounds and we start in the spectacular grounds of Traquair House with a cavalry charge for the main gates. A gentle downhill tarmac leads to a farm track leading onto the open hillside. This becomes more heathery and fernier before reaching the ridge and more good running before climbing Birkscairn Hill. Onwards to the heathery descent to cross Glensax Burn, to face a steep climb to Hundleshope and Stob Law. This steep heathery descent is where I was stopped in my tracks by a grotesque crack in my ankle when I stumbled down a rabbit hole, hidden by the heather. I tried to put weight on it after a minute but unfortunately it was too fragile. Nevertheless, I did not want a shameful mountain rescue call out so I hunkered down on hands with one leg in the air on my backside sliding down between the heather and rocks. David was running with me so when I was safely off Stob Law he ran along the track to the checkpoint, at Glenrath Farm, and alerted the first aid vehicle to come and collect me, stationed here for those wishing to withdraw. David had lost so much time ushering me safely off the hill that he most probably would have not made the cut-off time at the next checkpoint in Stobo. I had registered for another attempt in 2019 but it was a DNS (Did not Start).

Feel the Burns Hill Race, Selkirk 2018. The course was shortened because of the heavy snowfall. The course headed up through woodlands to join the forest track leading to Peat Law. Over snow covered moorlands towards the climb up to the Three Brethren then descending down the hillside to the drove track leading to Foulshiels Hill, what an exhilarating climb in very deep snow.

Foulshiels Hill, Feel the Burns Hill Race

Jan 2018 Devils Burden Relay, Gala Harriers put together a team for the Devils Burden. I had been allocated Leg 4, The Glory leg.

Leg 1: Falkland to Strathmiglo (single runner) 7.7km, 150m climb,
Leg 2: Strathmiglo to Kinnesswood (paired runners) 11.5km, 700m climb
Leg 3: Kinnesswood to Maspie Den (paired runners) 11.5km, 420m climb
Leg 4: Maspie Den to Falkland (single runner)

We all accompanied Eileen to the start at Falkland to whoop with encouragement before we clambered into the car to drive the changeover at Strathmiglo for the changeover to James and Neil (paired runners) to Kinnesswood. Then it was Kirsten, team captain, and her dad's turn, Ian, (paired runners) on the 3rd leg running from Kinnesswood to Maspie Den to my changeover in the woods. The top of East Lomond was not visible in the mist, however off I ran towards the summit meeting other runners descending, successfully avoiding collision. My map had disintegrated in the rain, I had not taken an outer map case to protect, mistake number one.

No sun, identical grey clouds mist and haar. There, almost at the summit, a walker had twisted their ankle and the marshal was attending to him. I heard a gate close so I decided, without checking on my soggy map, that was the way the runner in front had gone, visibility was too poor to actually see anyone. I did recall seeing a forest on my map but the one I was in seemed to be going on for a longer distance than anticipated. When back down into civilisation, there in a car was a man, with his dog, who assured me I was heading to Glenrothes and not Falkland. Glen, from Glenrothes, very kindly gave me a lift back to Falkland where I hung my head in shame upon meeting my team. DNF awarded.

Luckily my team mates saw the funny side of it and they all had their runs and did not burden me only ridiculed me for getting lost.

August 2018. Lomond Hills seems a nice wee hill run for this weekend's entertainment. Ignoring the fact that the race is entry on the day and we could have easily not gone as the weather was not in our favour. David and I set off in dreich, misty, rainy conditions to find a small field, only 60, a short race briefing on the start line that warned us strictly of no bum sliding off West Lomond due to slippery conditions but there is a first aid station at the bottom. Counted through as we start into the mist with all going well, up and down East Lomond but no views to be seen.

The field had spread out a bit and being in the mid-back pack, the only thing I could see was the faint outline of the person in front of me, making navigation difficult. Where is the steep descent we'd been warned about? Then as we reach the summit of West Lomond the marshal poked out from his shelter behind the trig point and yelled "follow the marked trail down". At first, I thought that doesn't look too bad, 90% gradient cliff. Contemplating the safest way down, I gingerly started walking down a section. Before I had the chance to decide the grass was so wet and long that I was almost immediately sliding down completely out of control unable to slow down or stop. I was in a panic and trying to dig my shoes into anything available, trying to turn on my side to grab grass to stop me! I must have slid past at least ten runners. It was quite honestly one of the most terrifying few minutes of my life. I managed to stop myself briefly, and staved thumb, in the process, when I saw David who had flipped over onto his stomach and sliding down headfirst. I promptly resumed my uncontrolled decent finally stopping myself near the foot of the hill. There was David who was checking if the guy in front of him was okay and he seemed to be okay.

Many went head first, some somersaulted, I was one of the lucky ones as at least two were taken to hospital, broken clavicle and stitches, what carnage. Oh how we nervously laughed, once over the trauma and relief to be at the bottom of the hill. All the marshals were busy administering first aid with the continuing havoc and we were too busy exchanging horrified stories that we did not pay much attention to where we were headed. After calming down and seeing no check point for a while this alerted us to our surroundings to which we checked our maps and confirmed we were heading in completely the wrong direction. We asked a farmer on a tractor if he knew, who more of less told us he couldn't care less as we come here every year wrecking everything and he was not too impressed at us running over his land. We worked it out ourselves and reported to the finish line but as we had not finished as per the route it was a DNF! Not sure if I am tempted to run it again. Coffee, cakes and some crisps at the Strathmiglo Village to ease the wounds.

Aug 2018. Glenshee 9 in the East Highlands, Scotland. In the run up to The Ring of Steall, David and I ran the Glenshee 9 continuing our training preparation focusing on leg strength, hill endurance as well as descent technique. A quick way to bag 9 munros. This is a Scottish Hill Race and only takes place every second year, comprising of 20 miles and 5,500ft run across the 9 Munro's bordering Glenshee Ski Centre in the East Highlands.

The race is run in an anticlockwise circuit across the following summits: - Creag Leacach (987m) Glas Maol (1068m) Cairn of Claise (1064m) Tom Buidhe (957m) Tolmount (958m) Carn an Tuirc (1019m) Carn Aosda (917m) Carn a'Gheoidh (975m) and The Cairnwell (933m)
Registration is in the Glenshee Ski Centre, 9 miles south of Braemar. Starts and finishes at Glenshee Ski Centre. The elevation is already 457m so it was not far to climb to summit the first Munro. The ground is rocky, heather, rubble and lots of tufty grass and after doing a couple of recces with a friend, Erni, I was confident of not getting lost. Very low-key race with a friendly registration boasting an exciting but slightly nervous atmosphere at the ski centre. The usual requirements to carry full body cover, whistle, map (this map must extend at least 2 km beyond your race route in all directions and be waterproof), compass and some emergency food, plus any additional

clothing dependent on the forecasted weather conditions. After being called through, counted then and a kit check we were off. It seemed like most of the field were happy to follow the leaders onto the first climb up to Creag Leacach which followed a narrow 'path' and onto open moorland. It was an anticlimax in reaching the Munro summit, a simple cairn tap and on we went. The next few tops involved some shorter ascents and steep downhills over the Heather laden Deeside hills.

Coming off Tolmount was a fast descent to the bealach followed by a long slog up to Carn an Tuirc. There is one road crossing after approximately 13 miles which is a checkpoint and is also a cut-off which must be reached within 4 hours of race start being strictly enforced.

The descent down to the road is a rocky and steep descent but a relief knowing I would secure the cut-off time, by 15 mins. Rewarded by the food supplies, we had previously hidden, It was a long 30min struggle up to Carn Aosda on steep heathery hill sides. I had to convince a fellow runner, sitting on the hillside, to continue as once up this final steep climb, the majority of the climbing was done. I continued to Carn a'Gheoidh (hill of the goose), finally doubling back to Cairnwell enjoying as it was perhaps the most runnable section. A short steep final descent from Cairnwell where you could see the finish line from the summit as runners followed the chairlift down which wasn't operating otherwise would have been an easier option.

Content feeling as I crossed the finish, with no expectations of my performance, I just enjoyed a day in the mountains. A phenomenal day out and fantastic race with great food provided at the cafe post-race! Finished in 5hr 35mins with WELL tenderised feet.

September 2018. Salomon, The Skyline Ring of Steall, 7,992ft / 17.6 miles (29km / 2,500m). Yearly, I like to have a main race to build up to and this year it was The Ring of Steall Skyrace and what a choice! Thank you to those who convinced me I could do it after many said WHAT?!

The Salomon Ring of Steall Skyrace is uncompromising mountain running, including scrambling up mountain ridges with steep ascents, traverses and descents on technical and challenging terrain. The weather was in our favour for this superbly organised European Organised Race with the route marked with orange flags to follow, there was tracking for friends and family to follow your progress and a well-stocked pit stop. Sometimes it is worth paying that bit extra to be spoilt and looked after. This time I had to convince David to do this race as our 2018 challenge and that it certainly was.

The race route is set on two lofty ridges within the Mamores and features some easy, but intimidating scrambling, including the Devil's Ridge, which provides a thrilling and airy traverse with Glen Nevis visible ahead and Ben Nevis beyond in the distance. The Ring of Steall consists of a horseshoe of Munros around Coire a Mhail from which the impressive Steall Waterfall cascades. The race starts and finishes in Kinlochleven on the West Highland Way path leading to The Devil's Ridge, with 5 checkpoints over the course.

The route traverses the An Gearanach ridge, a magnificent ridge extending north from the main spine of the Mamores, (Checkpoint 4) and Stob Coire a' Chairn (Checkpoint 5). The first ridge, there was a queue as competitors who had stopped to consider the correct hand and foot placements so as not to plummet off a cliff face. This rocky scramble can be avoided by taking a lower path but this was the marked route to follow. Poignant memories of this first ridge still haunt me, dramatically releasing my neck and shoulders from under my ears once I was up and running again. Many runners come from all over the world, to Scotland to get a real mountain challenge on not so beaten trails and wilder routes, offering stunning views, when the cloud lifts, with crystal clear air, cooling breezes and no midges. The world's finest mountain athlete was at the front of the start-line, Kilian Jornet, who took 20 mins off the previous record finishing in 3hrs 4mins... I was still on my way to Checkpoint 3 at Glen Nevis!

We wrongly started at the very back of the pack and with the race boasting over 700 participants creating a huge bottleneck at the WHW entrance which did not thin out until Checkpoint 3. Runners needed to be well ahead of the cut-off time at CP3 in order to complete the course which we both managed with ease. This was my first experience of mountain running following a route with red flags, even I could not get lost on this Salomon 29km steep, rocky, boggy, airy ridged Trail. Although I do not have a fear of heights, I ran with the attitude of keep going, don't look down as when I did, I stumbled every time I took my eyes off the path. At some point ascending someone was yelling "Rock", I was thinking, someone answer him please! then a large rock tumbled past me!

I passed many on the ascent then many passed me on my tentative descent. I had to stop and photograph what I'd accomplished, fortunately, the cloud had lifted to reveal a breath-taking view of The Devil's Ridge. The Glen Nevis Support point was welcome, the boiled potatoes and salt were such a hit which saved me bonking in the second half. Onwards and upwards again towards to the easier Munros of An Gearanach, Stob Choire a Chairn and Am Bodach back to meet up with the WHW to the finish line. David and I completed the race together attempting a sprint finish. Challenge complete, we headed to collect our gear from the registration centre and had the pleasure to meet Kilian Jornet who was in the queue to register for The Salomon Ben Nevis Ultra the next day.

Kilian Jornet at the Ring of Steall

October 2018. Pentland Skyline.
The Pentland Skyline is Category 'A' Long (AL) fell race covering 16 miles, 14 summits and 6200 feet of climb in the Pentland Hills on the

outskirts of Edinburgh with the first race being in 1986.

Taking part in this race is a serious commitment, your finish time will be on par with your road marathon time, 'they' say! The race route includes steep ascents and descents, on loose and rough ground and sections of difficult open moorland. The course is unmarked, you are expected to be able to navigate. That is the description from the race organisers, Carnethy Hill runners. Race day on Sunday morning was dry as we waited to register in the queue of the usual gluttons for their dose of sore muddy legs!

We all stood, on Caerketton, to be checked through making sure we had the SHR (Scottish Hill Racing) mandatory kit. The weather was kind with good visibility. Gun goes and we start on the trail leading to our first summit, a bottleneck is unavoidable on the narrow trail up the side of Caerketton forcing us to walk up. At the back of my mind was I had to get to West Kip, the 9th summit, before the cut off time of 2hrs 15 mins whilst staying alert to any hazards on the route. The churned up Drove Road, due to forestry operations, made Hare Hill seem easy terrain in comparison which is usually boggy.

Running! through the heather I glanced at my watch at 2hrs15m to see a few runners on the Kips who would have missed the strict cut off time. The descent off Hare Hill was a bit slippery as one guy demonstrated bum sliding down, not quite the same speed as Lomond of Fife Race the previous month, I was relieved to witness. Long trudge over Black Hill onto the steep ascent of Bell's Hill where stood, on the summit, the well-loved, Murdo McEwan who very kindly made me run round the back of him but gave me a jelly baby for doing so. My running buddy David kept cramping so he was reduced to walking and there limping up Harbour Hill was Luis Molero (Lauderdale Limpers) on the phone to his Girlfriend asking the millionaire question? "I've strained my hamstring, how do I get to the end of this race? - a) walk b) shameful Mountain Rescue c) cry?

They both struggled on together and finish we all did. Thank you, Carnethy Hill Running Club, for a well marshalled fun event. This was my second Skyline race where 251 started and 240 finished. I had entered for 2019, but unfortunately it was a DNS.

May 2019. Stuc a Chroin 5000. One of Scottish Hill Racing events and costs only £7 on the day to enter. Stuc is a cheeky wee race that is only a half marathon in distance with a few hills and bogs along the way. The 5000ft of ascent is the tough bit and certainly makes you work hard. I run the Stuc with a friend Simon Puttock who'd had a heart attack in 2017 but was now back running with strict heart rate monitoring regime managed to perfection.

The weather was reasonable, cold but clear with great views, dry which made the trail much less slippery with no snow to be seen but with the odd wee squall of mini hail stones to sting your face and arms. Never go off too fast that is key and Stuc gives you that opportunity with the first 5k along a forest track, slightly uphill, over a deer fence, continue to follow the fence on a narrow trail leading to a steep descent into Glen Ample displaying amazing view towards Beinn Each. Here you can envisage the extremely steep heathery climb to be endured to start the undulating ridge to Stuc a Chroin summit. Many marshals were there offering swigs of water and handfuls of jelly babies, I never really ate much of my own food and was 'all jelly babied out' by the descent. I drank the water to reduce the weight of my backpack but kept some as a security blanket! Plenty small burns around if a fill up was needed. We reached the summit of Stuc under the cut-off time with 15 mins to spare. The route off Beinn Each was a lovely grassy traverse, which allowed for decent running following the tape back to the deer fence and the forest track. Simon and I were running along the forest searching for the tape to turn to the finish, we must have overshot it as we spotted other runners coming back down towards us. They had done the same thing, we all turned back faffing around and finally took a turn into the forest and ended up on the road leading us back onto track spotting the finish line. Finlay Wild won for the 4th year with a PB.

May 2019. The Goatfell Hill Race, Brodick, Arran 2824ft, 15.5km. Although, Arran is a fair trip away from Edinburgh, the drive to the Ardrossan ferry is only about 1.5 hrs. This is followed by a relaxing 50 min boat crossing and you're in Brodick with only a short walk to the start. Easily done in a day with the race start and prize giving nicely organised around the ferry times. The Goatfell Race is classic with a bit of everything: road, trail, rough hill track, and scrambling up steep granite boulders to reach the dramatic summit. A tricky descent and fast return along the same road to Brodick where if you have anything left in your legs you can chase down scalps, which myself and another runner successfully did.

June 2019. The Lawers Group. One of the most popular mountain walking areas in Scotland, owing to the proximity of the Central Belt. Since I was getting much pleasure in 'running' Munros I started to bag a few more with a friend, Erni Hamilton and Dexter, her dog. We are fair weather Munro baggers and tend to conquest from April to September when our diaries agree. The Munro Trio had arranged another adventure, unfortunately weather was not glorious. The Lawers Group was the destination, ever so hopeful the mist would burn off. The Horn Carver Shop on Loch Tay owner, very kindly agreed to let us leave our car in the showroom car park, situated on the North side of Loch Tay, for a donation to Mountain Rescue. We were dropped off on the roadside to start our trail to Beinn Ghlas, where there were very few people ascending this Munro but when we reached the summit of Ben Lawers there were several people leading to a picnic playground at the summit, it was a Sunday after all! On towards An Stuc we left them all chattering and munching away! Two runners coming towards us stopped and chatted for a moment warning us of An Stuc descent. Erni negotiated Dexter down safely as we passed a terrified walker who was struggling down the cliff face with poles not doing her any favours. Next it was Meal Garbh and Meall Greigh following the old fence then descending following the Lawers Burn to a welcoming car. This was the last adventure for the Munro Trio for a while in the wake of Covid-19

July 2019 Lee Pen 5k Hill Race, St. Ronan's Border Games - Innerleithen's Festival. Scotland's Oldest Organised Sports Meeting, incorporating the Festival of St. Ronan Instituted in 1827. The Games are the oldest organised sports meeting in Scotland and are now part of a ten-day festival that incorporates many events for every age group. Central to the festivities are the Cleikum Ceremonies when the town's association with its Patron Saint, St. Ronan, is celebrated. According to the ancient story, St Ronan met the evil one and 'cleekit' him by the 'hint leg' and vanquished him with the only weapon to hand the Cleikum Crook. Lee Pen is a short Hill Race, 4.8km with a 350m climb, one lap of the games field, into the woods onto a grassy slope to steep climb up to the flag and back the way you came, through the ferns. There was a very small field which rewarded me with 3rd Female, the prize money, £10, in an envelope handed over to me at the finish line. Only £1 to enter, profit of £9

Saturday 27th July 2019. The Bikeless Beastie, was at Balloch Castle, Country Park, Loch Lomond for the 2019 Scottish National Aquathlon Championships, hosted by Lomond Swimming and Triathlon Club. I achieved a Podium place 3rd AG, but as I'm not Scottish Tri Affiliated, the 4th lady is enjoying my Bronze Scottish Triathlon medal. Two years ago, same story but I was 1st AG again no Gold Scottish Triathlon medal, need to affiliate! The weather was warm with the water temperature was 15°c so it was an optional wetsuit swim, but everyone chose to wear a wetsuit. The Scottish Aquathlon Championships and the Bikeless Beastie (same event) went off at 11:00am with 84 competitors doing a deep water start in Loch Lomond. The course was a

750m looped swim followed by a 5km run around the park finishing with an uphill sprint to finish line. With only a swim and a run, every aspect of the race was vital, including the long run up the slope from the jetty to transition and then transition itself.

July 2019. Moffat Gala Festival of Running 15k, (Moffat Devils Beef Tub), starts at 7pm with a field in excess of 170, obviously a rather popular race. Lots of English clubs and Borders Clubs were out in force. The race started with a very loud gun-fire, ringing in my ear for the first mile. The pace at the front looked very competitive, with the lead runners, shooting off. The course was marked every mile which, in contrast to hill races, is a nice structure for pacing yourself. The road undulated pleasant for the first four miles with the course not actually going anywhere near the Devil's Beef tub. Instead, at the four-mile mark and for almost a mile, we follow a steep track up to the A701. Pretty tough going, trying not to walk. The left road turn back to Moffat gives an amazing downhill, powerful finish. I was glad to reach the last mile entering Moffat, which was amazing to see the streets lined with people, cheering and clapping. What a wonderful atmosphere, additionally you get a cup of tea, a t-shirt, a Moffat Tea Coaster and a Mars bar. 1st Female Vet 50.

July 2019. Maddy Moss mid-week Bog and Burn race with a steep 2120ft ascent up The Law, the Ochil Hills. The race starts up a near vertical grass slope embellished with gorse bushes, before breaking onto a runnable path and a short rocky descent to a burn crossing. The ascent up the nose of The Law is significantly hands on knees, with only short sections of stumble running. The route opens out across the grassy tops of Ben Cleuch and Andrew Gannel Hill, before dropping down to a broad grassy ridge providing a great fast running descent leading onto a narrow track high above Gannel Burn. The final section of downhill is fast and technical before the near vertical plummet to the finish. My legs were a bit trashed from the Moffat 15k race the night before but an awesome hill race.

August 2019. The Ochil 2000's Category A, Long Series Hill Race! was the first of my three planned Category A Long Series Hill races planned for 2019. The Ochil 2000's is 21 miles in distance with a height gain of 5100ft, visiting every summit in the Ochil Hills measuring over 2000ft. Only two parts of the route are marked, from where to start onto the open ground below Innerdownie and then from the Gate at the entrance of Yellow Craig woods back to the University. On the course you have to search for the markers used in orienteering, orange style kite and punch or a Marshall at the summit of each of the 2000 foot plus peaks on the Ochil Hills and on the summit of Dumyat.

What else to do when celebrating 10 years since that bike accident 16th Aug 2009, pick a tough race and Simon agreed as he was celebrating two years since his heart attack. Simon always carries a GPS alarm in case of an incident in the hills which alerts mountain rescue, thankfully, he has never had to use it.

On the start line, there is an amazing connection in a group of diverse ages, nationalities, fitness levels etc setting out on a long hilly slog, especially as there is plenty of room for misadventure. Simon and I were dropped at registration, collected our race numbers, dibbers then ushered to the buses. That long journey round to Glendevon on the bus is enough time to give anyone the option to change their minds after realising you have to run back that distance.

It was a scorcher of a day with temperatures peaking at 25c making it extremely tough. The first 15 or so miles of the race were pleasant enough with no navigation disasters. Friends Jules and Peter were at the Maddy Moss checkpoint to cheer and support, always so motivational and encouraging to see friends whooping away. I encountered a few runners who had missed Ben Buck and were having to backtrack. I felt relieved that I had not done the same. The boggy bit over to Blairdennon was shorter than I remembered when doing the recce with Simon. Coming off Blairdennon I took some 'experimental' and interesting shortcuts off Myreton Hill which was a bit demoralising. The weather started to get a bit warmer, by Menstrie and I was starting to get those heavy legs. Several other runners bailed out at the last checkpoint choosing a lift back to the finish. I restocked up on water and sustenance from the table at the foot on Dumyat.

The drag up Dumyat was horrendous with next to no people around me now but I felt confident of the route to the finish, thank you Simon. Eventually, what seemed like a never-ending hill I was up and over Dumyat, thankfully not missing the turning to the woods, spotting the marking tape. Then there was that very special "last little bit" along the back of the university, which must actually be the best part of a mile, and feels like eternity. There were friendly faces and fruit at the finish. Simon was just behind me and we both collapsed in heaps on the grass.

We could allow ourselves a huge self-glorious satisfaction of job done completing in temperatures of 25°c, making it even tougher. 106 started 88 completed, several gave up at Dumyat.

12 Aug 2019. Bla Bheinn, Cuillin Ridge, Isle of Skye. Defeated by low cloud and rain to the summit of Bla Bheinn. This is one of the most magnificent mountains in Britain, a great isolated citadel of rock with fabulous views and all the character of the main Cuillin Ridge. Its ascent is straightforward by Cuillin standards but very rocky. From the summit, hikers have 360° views along the Cuillin Ridge and over the Isle of Skye, on a clear day. On the return journey home after running the Hebrides Marathon friend, Jules, and I decided to bag this Munro if the weather would let us. We spent ten minutes in the car waiting to see if the cloud would lift, we got lucky with breaks in the cloud and made a dash for it. For a hike like this, clear skies are not only ideal but necessary. As we approached the start of the hike, low clouds hung over the Cuillin Ridge. It was appealing to climb on a good path at first, with a river crossing but later the going becomes very rough, with loose stones, a scree gully, and some tough scrambling. These dark mountains are beautiful, even in the rain. This hike would take us to the summit of one of these mountains, letting me bag my first Cuillin Munro. Even though we could not see the summit, we decided to start the hike. Maybe we would get lucky and the skies would magically clear! Even if we could do part of the mountain, it would still be an adventure. I left Jules halfway up, spotted two climbers that I would attempt to catch up on but they

disappeared into the clag as I was scrambling up past Scree Gully. The Cloud didn't lift and I couldn't see two feet in front of me so sensible head, occasionally I do have one, was on and I climbed down. Spectacular is an understatement, overall, we had a fantastic experience.

The Ochil 2000's had been the first of my three Category A Long Hill Races for 2019. The Two Breweries and the Pentland Skyline were both planned but unfortunately a DNS (Did not Start) for both. So with two sorrowful unsuccessful attempts of the Two Breweries Race, one DNF (Did not Finish) and one DNS (Did not Start) this race is unfinished business, hopefully this year I will unburden myself of this load. I was ambitious to get to the start line and complete in 2020, Covid-19 permitting the race will be on. I was strong from days of running and racing in the hills when Simon announced he was going to run the Glenogle 33 Ultramarathon. I decided to join him, even although I had retired from Ultras. Unfortunately, again this was a DNS for myself and also Simon. I still have no intentions of returning to Ultramarathons.

5 THE STROKE

7am Saturday October 12th 2019 I am trying to push myself off the bedroom floor.

When I couldn't get up, I was thinking that had I overdone my upper-body training in the gym last night! But I knew there was something more seriously wrong than overexertion. I shouted out to my daughter, Jade, who came to my aid, luckily she was at home this morning as often stays over at David's house, her boyfriend, she could see clearly there was something wrong with me and immediately phoned 999 for an ambulance. Although I was in no pain, we were able to tell the call handler that it was a stroke I was having and an ambulance was dispatched immediately. I needed to go to the bathroom so poor Jade had to drag me to the toilet, putting a great strain on her back, it was a joint effort get me off the floor and onto the toilet seat. Jade was now extremely anxious and phoned her dad, Mo, telling him to come over to the house as soon as possible as mum has had a stroke, they followed the ambulance in their car. All this only took about 30 mins. When I arrived at the hospital, I was given an MRI scan which revealed a blood clot on the artery leading to the brain (Ischemic Stroke). Before I was given the miracle 'clot buster' drug Thrombolysis the Dr had to know exactly when the stroke started to decide whether safe to administer it or not. The 'clot-busting' drug is delivered through an intravenous (IV) line in your arm whilst heart and lung functions are monitored. The drug circulates within the blood stream until it reaches and disperses the clot. Within 30mins my facial droop had gone so had the numbness in my left arm and leg and I was able to wave to Jade and Mo, with my left arm, standing at the end of the hospital bed.

Recovery was going well, because I was in good shape and I had got to the hospital quickly. This improved my chances of full recovery, but only time will tell, how well and how quickly it would take to recover, was shocking to hear. It made me feel afraid and scared wondering what my future and my life was going to be like now.

No matter how fit you are stroke can happen to anyone, responding FAST can affect the recovery rate. FAST: - Face drooping - Arm weakness ~ Speech difficulty ~ Time to call 999

Reflecting on the days and events leading up

to the stroke as far back as September I had a really high temperature, felt dizzy and lethargic. David was wrongly accused for infecting me as I'd collected him and Jade from the airport, on their return from Majorca on the 5th September. He did have a temperature but from a bladder infection.

29th August, I ran my last road race before I had the stroke, The Media City 10k, Salford Quays, Manchester in 44:55, 1st place Age Group.

4th September I ran twice that day, three miles around Arthurs Seat and in the evening the Caerketton downhill race from the summit to the Car Park winning a box of Matchmakers chocolates for 2nd FV50.

5th, 6th & 7th September was the introduction to feeling lethargic, I was speculating it was from running twice in the same day.

8th I had arranged to do a Munro walk, The Ben Lawers range, with my friend Erni Hamilton. We went ahead with the plan and I half-heartedly ran five of Lawers group of Munros. We run whenever possible on our expeditions but this time I was reduced to several walking spates as a result of feeling lethargic.

On the 10th September I had a Doctor's appointment to have a physical examination to assess my overall condition, I was due to fly out to Lanazarote, Club la Santa on the 19th September. The Doctor observed and advised me to come back if symptoms got worse! I continued to feel unwell so I returned on the 17th September, this time the examination was more meticulous, blood was taken and blood pressure checked for hypertension, reading 150 / 80, (high systolic pressure). I was sent to have a chest x-ray the following day with a reassuring green light, all clear. I was phoned with the results of the blood tests, my liver was not functioning properly with the probability that I had Gallstones despite that I was not in pain and did not come into the bracket of those prone to gallstones: - fair, fat and forty. An ultrasound scan was to be arranged to confirm diagnosis, the Dr had no objections to me travelling on holiday.

11th September run aborted around the Braid hill as could not shake the feeling.

14th September I ran Vogrie Parkrun with Charlotte's daughter, Annabel age ten, who was attempting her first sub 30 min park run, she did effortlessly. Charlotte Hendry, Gala Harriers President was injured so I willingly ran with her, that was all the speed I could conjure up that day. A similar paced runner as myself, watching others as he had finished, remarked, 'what are you doing back here'.

17th September I struggled to run in the Pentland hills walking the last mile home

On the 19th September I flew out to Lanzarote starting to feel a bit better. The following morning, I joined the 5K Morning Run led by the Green Team managing to keep up a reasonable pace feeling I could breathe a bit easier. In the afternoon I had swim video analysis, I was given some stroke corrections to address and drills to help.

The following day 21st September I went up on a Volcanic Ridge, with a friend Jules for a run. We started on the road and headed up a ridge hill consisting of volcanic rock and sand. We ran up to and along the ridge then as we started the descent and were almost down, my left leg gave way. Jules described it as he saw it, as if I went down in slow motion. I started to get up to thinking I just had to brush the sand off, wrong! To my shock and horror, although not painful I could see the white bone of my Tibia. When I put my bodyweight on it, the blood ran like a river down my leg. I shouted at

Jules to give me his T-shirt so I could tie it around my leg to apply pressure on it to stop the excessive bleeding.

We had paused on the summit of the Ridge to admire the view and observed walkers below. Jules ran down to them to get help! They were extremely helpful and sympathetic, kitted with ample first aid supplies, yes unlike us! One lady phoned her husband who drove over to us in his 4x4 vehicle and took us back to Club La Santa. I went straight into the onsite Clinic where Dr Javier, a specialist in intensive care and the IRONMAN Doctor attended to my emergency. I am not squeamish, in the slightest, but I could not watch the procedure and sat upright on the couch with my arms folded over my eyes half in pain, half to shield the view of the operation. If you open your mouth and turn it vertical and fill it with loads of blood then that gives an insight to what it looked like. The wound was scrubbed to get the rock and granite out, several times, stitches internal, for the anterior tibialis fascia, then six external stitches to seal the wound. I was on his surgery table for a hour. Complicated wounds are almost guaranteed to be infected. That was me out of several hill races I'd entered much to my disappointment. The AZ

Sports Clinic based in Club la Santa, uses sport & science giving athletes information about their body's capacity and health carried out by doctors, it Is a busy clinic with injuries as well as advice.

Diagnosis as follows; Wide and deep incise contused wound, crescent shaped, around 8cm, on the anterior aspect or her right leg at the level of the tibial tuberosity, deep planes reach proximal tibialis anterior muscle which is exposed but not cut and periosteum close to tuberosity. After local anesthesia, thorough irrigation, brushing, cleansing the wound is sutured with absorbable stitches internal and 6 external to be removed in 12-14 days. Amoxicilina- clavulanico prescribed one 3 times per day.

That was the end of my all-inclusive sports week in Club La Santa becoming a basking in the sun recovery holiday. At first, I could not put any weight on my right leg and I had to limp and hobble around the resort with stairs being a huge challenge. With access to over 80 types of sports I took to watching the various classes and built up to walking 2:10 miles around the track in an hour before the end of the trip. I returned to the Clinic twice for the Dr to monitor the wound, he gave me a Tetanus vaccine and reported moderate swelling and stitches had mild tension, no discharge, no halo and to continue on Amoxicilina with a follow up visit to the GP when home.

We flew home on 26th September in discomfort as I could not bend my leg struggling to get comfortable. The flight was very busy as Thomas Cook had just gone into liquidation consequently, additional passengers on our flight lucky to acquire seats. I tried to move around as much as possible, the air stewards were first-class, allowing me to sit where the drinks trolley is positioned with my leg extended. Once home I made an appointment with the Dr to check the wound, he was not perturbed giving me a prescription extending the antibiotics for another week. After two weeks, I attempted to make an appointment to have the stitches removed, the receptionist advised that all the nurses were too busy that week and to phone back next week, I took the stitches out by myself.

Building up walking was going well, by 28th September, I was able to walk 3 miles with no repercussions thankfully. Although I was not going to run the Pentland Skyline race anymore, I had promised Simon I would take him for a recce of the route which I did on 3rd

October by dropping him at a point and following him in the car. The race was on the 13th October.

9th October I went for the Ultrasound Scan to determine whether it was gallstones or not. No gallstones or inflammation of the gall bladder and referred back to the Doctor, needless to say I was ecstatic. With my health improving apart from the knee injury I started going to the gym again for upper body drills on TRX bands until the knee mended. Before I got the chance to contact the Doctor, for further advice, it was on the 12th October I had the Stroke.

A stroke happens when the blood supply to part of the brain is interrupted. In my case it was a blood clot, as a result brain cells get less of the oxygen and nutrients that they need. Ischaemic stroke occurs when a blood clot blocks one of the arteries that carries blood to the brain, the majority of strokes are ischaemic. For most, a stroke happens without warning, however some people do experience symptoms such as dizziness, loss of balance, changes in vision etc. High blood pressure, over a period of time, is the number one risk factor for stroke, I usually have very low blood pressure hence why it was a shock for me to record 150/80 in the Dr surgery that day.

A stroke is investigated to get to the root of the cause, mainly to try and avoid a secondary stroke. I had the Echocardiogram test which is an ultrasound scan used to analyse how blood flows through the surrounding vessels on the heart. My neck was also tested with a carotid doppler, an ultrasound test, to examine the carotid arteries located in the neck. This can show narrowing or possible blockages due to plaque build-up in the arteries, nothing was detected, all clear. Next was the five-day electrocardiogram (ECG), a test used to check the heart's rhythm and electrical activity. Sensors are attached to the skin, to detect the electrical signals produced by the heart each time it beats. These signals are recorded by a machine and are looked at by the specialist to see if they're unusual. The ECG can help detect arrhythmias, where the heart beats too slowly, too quickly or irregularly. The small, sticky sensors, electrodes, are attached to your chest which are worn for five days. These are connected by wires to an ECG recording machine. Limited showers for 5 days. The results came back as reassuringly normal sinus rhythm.

From all the testing nothing was detected as to what caused the stroke. I was prescribed

Clopidogrel, a blood thinner that makes your blood flow through your veins more easily making the blood less likely to make a dangerous blood clot, having an increased risk of having them.

I was in the Stroke Ward in the Edinburgh Royal Infirmary along with another three older ladies who were in their seventies and eighties. It is just a horrendous experience being in hospital not able to fend for yourself when you are used to being independent then it is suddenly taken away from you. I phoned my son, Ryan 16yrs, from the hospital who had slept through all the commotion, he had stayed at his dads' house that evening. He was surprised to hear me telling him I was in hospital having had a stroke and to come in and visit.

Although the Doctors were pleased with my progress, I was not allowed to go home unless the Physio and Occupational Therapist authorised it. I was slowly becoming aware of what had happened, it was now the decisions of Physicians to decide my state of health. I was not allowed to go to the toilet alone, I had to press the buzzer for a nurse to take me, to make sure I did not fall and haemorrhage as a result of the amount of blood thinners I had been given. I can remember how daunting it was to go to the toilet, for the first time by myself in the hospital ward unaided holding onto the furniture as I went along, but with sheer determination I wanted to prove I could do it, seeing it as a step closer to getting home. After a few visits to the bathroom and being allowed to take a shower by myself I slowly gained confidence and developed it. Next step was the physio taking me for a few steps to the door of the ward room and back unaided.

I had now been in the hospital for two days and I was to be tested by the physiotherapist to see if I was capable of walking up and down the stairs, walk in straight lines, stand on one leg etc. I was confident going upstairs but very apprehensive of going down the steps. Then it was onto Occupational Therapy with their tests, draw me a clock she says and draw me ten past eleven, so I did with the numbers on the outside of the circle. She asked me where do you usually draw the numbers on a clock? I reply 'I don't usually draw clocks'! I think I got a mark for cheek on that question. On the bright side they all agreed that I could leave the hospital with words of warning take it easy for the next 3 weeks as that's the most likely time for the recurrence of a stroke.

I was determined to get back out running again, one of the main questions I asked the specialist was "will I be okay to train for the London marathon?" He asked when it was. I had two months to build up my walking to running to start a training programme in two months. I had a great team of doctors and therapists and with my mindset I knew there was a lot of work ahead of me to start running again from being taken to the toilet in a commode, furniture walking and walking out the hospital.

I was discharged on 15th October suffering from post-stroke fatigue, where your body is recovering from a sudden event. Having a stroke had a huge impact on my life. all of a sudden, I was very anxious about going out for a walk by myself, let alone a run. I made sure I had a friend to accompany me when I first started walking. On my first venture, not even one mile I only made it to the park near my house, next day at bit further and following day a bit further and so on until I managed around the park.

By 23rd October I could walk just over 1 mile, I found it daunting to go into a café. My friend Gloria, who is a nurse, was aware of this and would pick me up and we would drive to

Flotterstone area of the Pentlands to go for a walk and then into the café for lunch to reinstall being comfortable around other people. Family and friends would remark to Jade 'thank goodness you were there' which had a powerful impact on her making her think 'what if I hadn't been' and was and still is a bit reluctant to leave me in the house on my own and ensuring her brother Ryan is at home whenever she stays at David's house.

By the end of October, I was walking up to three miles daily and looking forward to meeting up with friends. I continued this way and when finally, I had the courage to walk alone I started to introduce jogging into my routine. By November I slowly prolonged the jog / walk until I could run 3 miles. We went on a family holiday to Aviemore 17th November where I relived the Lairig Ghru finish albeit very slowly. I attempted my first swim in the hotel pool and it took me 14 mins to swim 500m which used to take 10mins. By mid November I was running 4 times per week very cautiously and slowly with the occasional swim.

1st December I ran in my first race after the stroke at the Borders Cross Country Series, Spittal Beach, Berwick Upon Tweed. The route was a mix of hard then very soft deep sand, with steps up onto the headland which was undulating grass and track. It was an out and back route, the sand was tough going, as was the -2 cold sea breeze! My running club Gala Harriers were very supportive that day and surprised to see me back in a race. Later that week as I continued my confidence building, I successfully ran walked up and over the Kips in the Pentlands in the mist.

7th December I went back for my first park run at Vogrie Park and completed in 25:38, my PB for Vogrie Park run is 21:56. By now I was upping the mileage with London training looming and now at 10 miles for my long run.

15th December Peebles Cross Country I was 4:35 mins slower than last year. I improved Vogrie Park run by 40 seconds. Claire Dalrymple, my marathon running friend, took me out on a 13-mile route she had measured and I took a tumble on uneven slabs at Duddingston Park jarring my right arm and opening the cut on my right knee just as it was all healing perfectly.

2nd January I went on the yearly Gala Harriers and Lauderdale Limpers annual Ice Breaker from Lauder to Melrose across the Southern Upland Way, Eileen Maxwell very kindly stayed with me. There is great camaraderie between these Borders Running Clubs and nothing like a fried egg roll after braving the elements of a strong headwind.

As my confidence developed, I continued with my training for London Marathon incorporating park runs at the weekend alternating with Cross Country races.

18th January Scottish Athletics East District, Cross Country in Livingston the Gala Harries Masters girls, myself, Lyndsay Dunn and Eileen Maxwell placed 3rd.

8th February The venue for this year's edition of the Scottish Athletics National Masters Cross-Country Championships was in Johnstone, west of Glasgow.

The event featured two races, with the Women (W40 and above) and Men (M65 and above) racing over 6 Km, followed by Men (M40 to M60) racing over 8 Km. Although both races were completed before the full effect of the forecast storms were seen, a mixture of an undulating course with heavy underfoot conditions in parts and a stiff breeze meant for a tough challenge. Runners were eligible for individual medals in five-year age categories and also team medals in either the 40-50 age category or 50 years and above. Gala Harriers fielded teams in both the Women's team categories and were desperately unlucky to miss out on the medal positions, finishing 4th team overall in both categories. The W50+ team for Gala Harriers ran an excellent race, missing team bronze by only a few points. Myself and Lindsay Dun supported each other well, racing in close contact throughout with Lyndsay finishing 55th overall (7th W50) and myself 56th overall (5th W55). Eileen Maxwell finished close behind in 85th overall (9th W55) to complete the team. The men ran well, four runners were required to count in the Men's M40-M50 team competition, with Gala Harriers eventually placing a creditable 7th. The team were led home by Graeme Murdoch (36th overall, 19th M40) and Gary Trewartha (41st overall, 21st M40). Sprinting together down the finishing straight were Magnus Inglis (120th overall, 38th M40) and Colin McCall (122nd overall, 34th M45) to complete the team placings. Bob Johnson ran a typically strong race in the M60 category to finish 135th overall, 13th M60.

15th Feb Livingston park run, still not quite broken 23 mins yet but getting closer, 23:02 this time!

22nd February The National Cross-Country

Championships at the now traditional venue of Callender Park in Falkirk. The highlight of the XC racing calendar, the National Championships feature the best endurance running talent in the country competing in 10 races across the age-groups. Gala Harriers were represented in most of the races. The weather and ground conditions prior to the event had required some last-minute changes to the intended course maps, and a day of horrendous weather which included strong winds, snow, hail, rain and some sunshine meant all athletes faced a tough challenge to stay upright and finish their race. It was a wonderful tough mudfest which I placed 2nd FV55 proving I am well and truly on the mend.

1st March Lasswade 10 I do this race yearly and unknown to me at the time it would be my last road race for a long time. The race comprises of a 10-mile loop set in a scenic, rural location, run mainly on road. It starts at the west of Rosewell village, the route follows a gentle incline to Gourlaw Farm before dropping down to the bottom of Roslin Glen at two miles, followed by a steep rise for 400 metres. After there it should have been a nice and easy run until storm Jorge dropped off two months of rain overnight turning the road into a stream. The options were either wade through it or join the queue with other runners for the grass verge to avoid wet feet. The four-mile mark is in the village of Auchendinny, then there is a climb between the fifth and six miles and thereafter, apart from a short incline at around seven miles. The route is generally downhill into Rosewell. If you had opted to keep your feet dry at the last road stream there was no option at mile 9, you had to go through the flooded trail path which was up to your knees. Again 4 mins slower than last years' result.

8th March the following Sunday was Chirnside Cross Country the presentation round of the Borders series Cross Country where you are presented with your medal and refreshments. This was not only the last Cross-Country Race of the season it was my last race for a while due to Covid-19. I was up to running 20 miles on my long run now which I had run five times when it was announced on 15th March that the London Marathon was being postponed until October 4th 2020.

14th March was the last park run at Vogrie, due to Covid-19, finishing in 23:36 still nowhere near breaking the 23mins.

It was end of November I ventured back to swimming in a 25m pool and really struggled. My front crawl average strokes in a 25m pool length was 22, I was now taking 32 strokes and 40 seconds instead 30 seconds per length. This prompted me to contact the physiotherapist who specialise in stroke casualties. The Physio detected I have a weakness in my left shoulder girdle and gave me a personal exercise programme to strengthen it with using body weight. I had progressed to using weights in the gym but with COVID-19 the gym closed. I have also a slight weakness in my left leg.

My voice was also affected, I struggled to speak loudly, clearly and confidently. I attended a speech therapist, learning how to speak again, this helped immensely with my confidence. By practising breathing patterns you can gain control over your breath to develop a stronger voice. I was coached several times learning to project my voice by slowing down and over emphasizing. Although now my voice is much more powerful, I still am guilty of trying to say too much in one sentence and gasp for air at the end.

Resilience is the psychological quality that allows some people to be knocked down by the adversities of life and to come back strongly. Rather than letting difficulties, traumatic events, or failure overcome you and drain your resolve, be highly resilient and find a way to change course, heal emotionally, and continue to move towards goals.

Raising resilience, there is a way to overcome major setbacks, upsets and disappointments. This can all be enforced by being more resilient within yourself, we all need a bit perseverance, grit and determination to overcome any setbacks, believe in yourself and accept that a challenge is achievable, never be afraid of failing, try and try again until you succeed until it is your own accomplishment.

The London Marathon was cancelled and went ahead only for the Elite runners. Virgin arranged a Virtual London Marathon on October 4th 2020. To coincide with this and as it was approaching one year since my stroke I measured, organised and ran a marathon with a few friends, due to the covid-19 restrictions, across the Pentland Hills. It started from Robert Louis Stevenson's 'cockmylane' path and ended at Blackmount Church in Dolphinton, 26.2 miles with 4967ft ascent and 10 peaks, taking us 6hrs 33mins. My story started to spread in the News as Angie Brown had written an article for the BBC online about the Pentland Marathon. Other media became interested and magazines. It came to a pinnacle with a BBC interview with Heather Dewar TV Sports Presenter during the Live London Marathon. I was a feature during the Men's Elite race on Gabby Logans highlights from the Virtual London Marathon 2020. Heather interviewed me just as we were starting off on our adventure giving the history of my stroke and my reason of running to raise funds for Chest Heart Stroke Scotland. I raised £1600 and raised awareness that a stroke can happen to anyone even fit individuals, with no obvious risk factors that don't smoke, eat healthily and kept fit.

I decided to put the same determination to my love of running into my recovery from the stroke.

It was an arduous process and still is, both physically and mentally with a physiotherapist helping to learn to strengthen weaknesses and a speech therapist teaching me to speak again, mindset is important and believe in yourself "that if anyone can do this, I can." We only get one chance: -

One   Life   —   Live   It

6 COVID-19 VIRTUAL RACES

2020 what a disastrous year with COVID-19 taking over the world. Stay at home, protect the NHS, save lives, keep two metres apart to avoid catching or spreading the virus. You are safe if you maintain social distance when out but you can't go out with friends, walking running or cycling as it may result in life imprisonment!!! So many confusing conflicting stories went around, it was hard to believe any, apart from it destroyed our races year and with the majority of businesses forced to close down over the country myself included.

That put a stop to all Physiotherapy and Speech Therapist sessions I was attending. The were NHS cancelling appointments to ensure that the staff were available to take care of the most vulnerable patients. My Physio, Katie, had found a weakness in the left shoulder girdle after I visited her complaining that my swimming was awful since the stroke. I used to swim a 25m length in 22 arm strokes it was now taking me 32 strokes as no strength in the pull-back phase. This was all part of the stroke, but I am determined to strengthen it up again. Katie very kindly e-mailed a Personal Exercise Program to continue exercises at home. I had been using weights in the gym but with all gyms now closed there was no access to equipment. I also had exercises for my right knee to strengthen the quads to try and reduce the pressure on the scar on my knee from the Lanzarote fall which was protruding like a second kneecap. The Speech Therapy was almost at an end and I was discharged with notes on Dysarthria Techniques to continue practicing at home to strengthen my voice. It was working amazingly well and my voice is 80% back to normal now.

I had been training hard for the London Marathon and working on endurance rather than speed and already ran five 20 milers by 15th March. That was when we received the e-mail informing us that London Marathon is postponed and rescheduled to take place on 4th October. Very disappointing for so many runners and the thousands of charities for which we raise money. As I write although the race has been rescheduled many are unsure it will go ahead in October as the UK has still not reached the peak of the pandemic. That put an end to the weekly long run but I still had races booked in the lead up to London but inevitably they were cancelled, postponed or rescheduled for later on in the season or next year. Like everyone else, my racing plans for the spring had been decimated leaving a huge void, in all runners lives.

23rd March saw the UK going into Lockdown being reviewed every 3 weeks by the government. No need to do any further 20-mile road runs so I took to the Pentlands as the weather had been improving.

Beginning of April 2020, on my weekly long run in the Pentlands, there on Castlelaw descent I spotted a friend, I'm sure we are stalking each other as there she was again. We had a safe distance walk and chat then I continued up to Allermuir and Caerketton. Once safely down the peaks running towards the Icelandic Ponies my right foot slipped in the dry scree and I hit the ground with a heavy fall busting my knee, yet again! I heard the stone slice into my forehead as I hit the ground and knew it wasn't good, blood ran down into my eye as I stood up. Luckily, I had emergency kit in my backpack and it was only about a mile to home so I continued to run holding onto the bandage compressing the blood flow. Adrenalin surged as I ran home looking like something from a horror movie. Parents pulled their kids out the way in case I scared them rather than catch COVID-19! Forehead could do with a stitch or two but in present time I didn't bother the NHS so I tended to it myself with surgical spirits and butterfly stitches...another scar to add to the collection. Two weeks later fractured ribs confirmed as the pain when sneezing, coughing and laughing was just not getting any better. WORST thing is I cracked the screen on my Garmin watch.

Scottish Athletics is the national governing body for athletics in Scotland, established in 2001, they piloted Virtual Races to those who were SAL registered. Over the Easter weekend, April 11th, Scottish Athletics hosted a Virtual Road Relay Challenge. Respecting current running guidelines, the event followed as closely as possible the format of the National 6/4 Stage Road Relay Champs. Athletes completed either a 5K or 10K solo run and then uploaded their results via Strava/Garmin. For the Senior races the fastest 3 times from both the 5K and 10K distances counted towards the 6-person team score, with the Masters (over 50) event consisting of 2 times of 5K and 10K each. There was an excellent response from Gala Harriers for this event, with a large number of strong results being posted over the weekend. The Green

Machine, Gala Harriers, finished with a Top 10 placing in all categories contested, but Gala Harriers conveyed a special mention to the Women's Masters team who raced their way to the podium and a (virtual) silver team medal. It is good strengthening for a fractured rib to breathe deeply. Charlotte Hendry is the current president of Gala Harries who does an amazing job with her bubbly personality and friendly warmth, she has threatened to wrap me in bubble wrap before I head out running!

Women's Masters category, 2nd team out of 8:

2:30:52 for 30K total: Eileen Maxwell (23:46, 5K), Jocelyn Richard (23:55, 5K), Carole Fortune (48:40, 10K), Eileen Nicol (54:31, 10K)

Women's category, 7th team out of 24:

3:07:10 for 45K total: Jennifer Forbes (19:25, 5K), Katie Rourke (20:03, 5K), Julia Johnstone (20:39, 5K), Zoe Pflug (38:42, 10K), Kirstin Maxwell (39:41, 10K), Carole Fortune (48:40, 10K)

Men's category, 9th team out of 33:

2:35:05 for 45K total: Gary Trewartha (16:47, 5K), Graeme Murdoch (17:07, 5K), Brian Aitchison (17:45, 5K), Marcus D'Agrosa (32:53,

10K), Darrell Hastie (33:15, 10K), Clark Scott (37:18, 10K)

Many organisations and clubs continued the trend of Virtual races and on Easter weekend Gala Harriers hosted a virtual Easter 5K. where we were all winners and received a virtual Easter Egg.

The next Scottish Athletics Virtual Challenge was on the weekend of April 24-27 where athletes 'go the distance' for your club in a 15-Minute Challenge – while observing social distance guidelines. For the 15-Minute Challenge there were four different scoring categories, with athletes and clubs required to upload distances (in kilometres) via Garmin/Strava by noon on Tuesday 28 April

All distances from all runners in each age group category count towards the overall club's distance for U13, U15, U17, U20, Senior and Masters. Every extra kilometre counts in this total club distance category, which adds up the distances run by all members of from U17 and above and genders to give one overall total for your club. Over 1100 athletes took part and Gala Harriers placed 8th team overall out of 70, with the juniors placing 4th out of 45 overall. Gala used this event as a Fundraising Opportunity and raised £400 for NHS Borders.

The next latest Virtual Challenge organised by Scottish Athletics featured the 1-Mile Time Trial over the weekend of 8th-11th May. This was the third Scottish Athletics event in the Virtual Challenge series and once again proved hugely popular with approximately 1247 finishes for the mile solo runs. All runs were completed according to current guidelines and were required to feature no net elevation loss to ensure as fair a comparison between runners as possible. Gala Harriers were out in force again for this challenge, with 39 members of the Green Machine from U/13 to Masters age groups taking on the 1-mile distance. All athletes went after the challenge with the usual Gala grit and there were some stand-out times posted. The Women's 'A' team of Kirstin Maxwell (5:34), Julia Johnstone (6:03), Lindsay Dun (6:33) and Erin Gray (6:37) were 17th team out of 89, with the Masters Women's 'A' team of Julia Johnstone (6:03), Lindsay Dun (6:33), Eileen Maxwell (6:44) and Carole Fortune (6:46) placing an excellent 4th out of 29 teams.

Scottish Athletics, Club in Focus section, there was an excellent article by Katy Barden on the growth of Gala Harriers:

'Arthur Conan Doyle, creator of Sherlock Holmes, was one of the original patrons of Gala Harriers when the club was formed in

1902.

When the club celebrated its centenary in 2002, former Scotland Manager Craig Brown was a guest speaker and shared his own stories – less criminal and more celebratory. He remains the last Scotland Manager to steer his team to a major tournament (FIFA World Cup, France 1998).

In spite of its famous connections, however, Gala Harriers is less about status and more about driving participation. Any success is a bi-product of the efforts of athletes and club officials.

From its early male-dominated days, it has evolved from a primarily road and cross-country club to an all-encompassing athletics club, a move driven in part by the growth of its junior section from the early 2000s.

'We had a handful of junior members to begin with, but now we have more than 100 junior members which is almost half of our total club membership,' says Neil Renton, the club's Head Coach.

'The introduction of our junior section has made us think and act differently. We were historically an endurance club but not all kids are endurance athletes, so we had to adapt.

'We've also developed an effective coaching structure to support the numbers of athletes we're working with.'

More of the article can be read
https://www.scottishathletics.org.uk/55012-2/

Gary Trewartha, not only is he one of Gala's speedsters he is an excellent report writer, constantly compiling round-up reports of the 'Green Machines' racing activities. I have used a lot of his reports throughout this journal. Gary introduced a new challenge to the club.

Gala Harriers Grand Prix 2020 (GP2020)

The intention of GP2020 is to generate some light-hearted competition within the club and possibly encourage athletes to enter races they might otherwise not have entered, going out of your comfort zone if you like.
In each month January-November a race has been nominated where GP2020 points will be on offer. Points will be awarded for each race depending on your Gala Harriers finishing position.
A mix of road, trail, XC and hill races have been selected.
Updates will be sent out on the Club's Facebook page (the closed one) and also the club website, including race info, upcoming entry deadlines, race results and latest standings.

The last race in the 2020 series will be the annual Club XC Champs, with the intention to crown the GP 2020 Champion later that day at the prizegiving evening.

Grand Prix after 3 events is all on hold due to Covid-19

Covid-19 dragged on and on and many different opinions started to appear from all over the world as countries succumbed to and recovered. The Public were monitoring the impact of the pandemic within their countries and beyond the European Union. The crisis and the measures taken on all levels to contain it had significant implications on citizens' perception and expectations of their governments.

We all have very varied opinions of Coronavirus and the view that I leaned towards was: - that the virus is likely to change quickly, with less virulent forms becoming dominant. Lockdown could potentially slow this beneficial tendency. On this view, asymptomatic people spreading the virus is a good thing because it means that the disease becomes milder more quickly. This could already be contributing to the flattening of the reported deaths curves. This suggested, the sooner we lift lockdown, the better. It also implies that the peak in illnesses we have seen this time around is likely to be as bad as it gets. In future, the virus will come into equilibrium with the population as wider immunity combines with milder forms of the virus to cause a lower overall death rate that nevertheless fluctuates from year to year, much like flu.

Many countries with very different approaches to lockdown seem to have similar curves, their different testing and recording of the virus allows meaningful comparison. Are the curves a result of our actions or are they just a manifestation of the way this virus is coming into equilibrium with its new human hosts? The curves on those affected by the virus seem similar to the population curves as well. It's easy make arguments that what we are doing 'must' be slowing the spread.

The economic and health costs of lockdown are enormous. Lockdown has caused huge disruption to healthcare of conditions other than Covid-19, which is having significant effects and will also have significant delayed effects on other illnesses and deaths. The direct health effects of lockdown and economic downturn have an unreasonable effect on younger people with more longevity, so comparing deaths between Covid-19 and other causes such a suicide does not do justice to the scale of the health effects attributable to lockdown. Factor in all the lockdown mental and physical health effects it is obvious that lockdown is having a huge impact on the quality of life across the population that far outweighs those caused by Covid-19.

No one thinks this virus will be eradicated and we should learn to live with it as we have with other major viruses. David Attenborough's virus documentary was very informative asking the question are humans responsible for the impact we are having on our planet with our destructive relationship with nature and pandemic diseases. It will always be within the population and will spread in its own way. The impact of this pathogen will be measured, like flu, over years where some years are worse than others. Our own immune systems have been sharpened by millions of years of evolution to cope with viral threats. They are the way we survive in a world full of viral pathogens, many of which we have all already had without knowing. Countries that now have a low incidence of the virus will have to face it later. The virus may enter on the wind, pets, or some other way that has not yet been discovered. No country has ever improved the health of its population by making itself poorer. Lockdowns are impairing our ability to live with the effects of this virus. Coronavirus affects mainly the elderly and those with pre-existing conditions. But the large majority of people who catch the disease recover. In the meantime, lockdown is preventing many of the things that make life worth living: seeing children, grandchildren, and friends; eating out, hobbies, charity work, travelling. Doing all the things that people work so hard to be able to enjoy. Isolation is dangerous for everyone but particularly the elderly. When we reflect back in years to come, we will see the damage that it has caused.

Lockdown directly harms those who will be largely unaffected by coronavirus the vast majority of people under 65, and almost everyone under 50, will be no more inconvenienced by this disease than by a cold unless they have an underlying condition. They are being asked to make huge sacrifices for something that will not affect them. Education, jobs, businesses: these are not abstract concepts, they are people's lives. This group includes the people who are the most productive part of our society and whose efforts support everyone else, including those who are ill. The argument that they might unknowingly pass the virus on to others and so are best to stay at home – the 'stay at home, save lives' message given to us by government. Lost education, lost job opportunities, and destroyed livelihoods and childhoods cannot necessarily be made good. The health service has not been overwhelmed and has, thankfully adapted quickly.

Report on the Scottish Athletics Challenge
written by Gary Thewertha;

*'Gala Harriers athletes were once again out in
force to participate in the latest virtual
challenge organised by Scottish Athletics. This
time the focus was a Club Distance Challenge
with athletes given the option of completing
either 15- or 30-minutes of running and
recording their total distance covered. Younger
athletes were limited to the 15-minute run.*

*The excellent level of participation was evident
in the club rankings, with Gala Harriers placed
5th of clubs nationally in the Under-17 and
above categories and a superb 4th placed club
in the Under-13/15 category. In the team
rankings for the 15-minute challenge, there
was a brilliant 2nd place overall. In the team
rankings for the 30-minute challenge, the 'A'
team placed 3rd overall.*

*A number of Gala Harriers featured strongly in
the individual rankings, with the following
athletes running superbly to place in the top 10
nationally for their respective age groups:*

*15-minute challenge - Zico Field 7th U13B,
Jennifer Forbes 2nd W45, David Nightingale*

*6th M60, Lindsay Dun 1st W50, Eileen Maxwell
2nd W55, Lisa Dalgliesh 9th W45, Carole
Fortune 4th W55.*

*Hopefully the excellent levels of involvement
from the Gala Harrier athletes in the recent
virtual challenges will put the club in a good
position when real racing can re-start.*

Mid-June was a busy weekend for Virtual
Races with four in the same weekend. June
2020 was the first SA virtual Hill Race to be
completed between Friday 19th June and
Monday 22 June. The challenge is to climb as
many vertical metres as possible in 30 minutes
(U17 to Masters) and 15 mins (U13 to U15).
Runners use a slope or hill in their local area
and record their total vertical ascent and
descent. The challenge can be completed like
hill reps or as a hilly run, planning the run to
have as much vertical ascent as possible. The
maximum ascent for one climb should be
approximately 100m. The total ascent and
descent should be approx. the same. Scoring
Categories Total Climb by Individual Age and
Gender This category ranks individual athletes
in each age group and gender category
running the most metres in 30 minutes (U17 to
Masters) and 15 mins (U13 to U15). Every
extra metre count in the total club climb

category, which adds up the climbs run by all members of all ages and genders to give one club total. C In the team categories, the most metres climbed over each 30 min run by athletes from the same club will contribute to the 'A' team. The next best results will make up the club's 'B' team, and so on to include all athletes competing. 1 attempt per person.

VIRTUAL West Highland Way Race
Sunday 21st June 2020

Having previously run the West Highland Way in 2015 I never gave it a second thought about running it again until I had the chance to do it as a part of a team and virtually. The 95 miles (155km) distance of the West Highland Way, Scotland's iconic long-distance trail, like all virtual events, it relied on honesty from everyone just getting out there, logging the miles as accurately as possible, and having a bit fun too.

The event Starts Midnight Thursday 11th June and ends midday Sunday 21st June. Runners had 9.5 days to complete the 95 miles. It strongly discouraged anyone from running 95 miles in one go. The virtual run allowed runners to run 95 miles, over 9.5 days, either individually, as a semi competitive 3 runner team relay, or as a multi team fun relay.

We chose the multi team fun relay with segments of our choosing which were completed by each of the 3-checkpoint cut off deadlines.

Checkpoints at:

Inversnaid - Leg 1: Total 36 miles that must be completed by midnight **Mon 15th June**

Victoria Bridge - Leg 2: 27 miles, total 63 miles to be completed by midnight **Thurs 18th June**

Fort William - Leg 3: 32 miles giving a total of 95 miles to be completed midday **Sun 21st June**

After we completed the leg the time was recorded. Once the deadline for completing each leg has passed, the cumulative time and position on the Results webpage was displayed

West Highland Way race is a not for profit event, run by volunteers. The cost of entry was very low and any surplus funds were donated to Scotland Association for Mental Health. Gala Guys n Dolls placed 4th out of 84 Teams

The same weekend it was; The British Masters Virtual 5k Relays

Sunday 14 Jun 2020 3 stages of 5km for all women Over-35 and men Over-55; 4 stages of 5km for men Over-45; and 6 stages of 5km for men Over-35. Athletes will choose their own 5km course and run this between 14th and 20th June 2020. They will record their own time and distance using an electronic device, and enter the URL of their result into the results system.

British Success for Gala Women!

'Once again the Gala Ladies show the way with winning performances for the Scottish region in the recent British Masters Athletics Virtual 5km Relays.'

Huge congratulations to Julie Johnstone, Lisa Gregg and Angela Jewitt for placing 1st W45-54 team in the Scottish section of the relays.

Also, a massive well done to Carole Fortune, Eileen Maxwell and Jocelyn Richard

for placing 1st W55-64 team in the Scottish section of the relays.

Carole Fortune 3rd W55-64

A copy of the winner's certificate was emailed to us.

Hopefully we are nearing the end of virtual races and getting back to real races in the near future. The latest virtual race I entered was the Great North Run. I've never run the GNR or attempted to gain a place in it as I feel it is oversubscribed and overpriced for a half a marathon, but another 'famous' race medal to add to the collection.

We are now in July 2020 with the only races taken place are virtual but Scottish Athletics have made an announcement for races to re commence on 1st August 2020 complying to Covid-19 guideline

On June 24th my friend Claire Dalrymple and I went out and ran the 7 hills of Edinburgh Race just for pleasure at our own pace. The race takes place annually with the course being a combination of road-running, cross-country, hill-running, and urban orienteering. The total distance is advertised as little over 14 miles, we totalled 17! with about 2200 feet of ascent, our elevation gain was 2600ft. There are many road-crossings and self-navigation is involved. The race starts at Calton Hill, we started at Braid Hill to avoid transport complications. In the race competitors have to find their own route, the course is not marked and has 6 checkpoints to punch their race-number with clippers): -

- The Castle (esplanade)
- Corstorphine Hill
- Craiglockhart Hill (East)
- Braid Hill
- Blackford Hill
- Arthur's Seat

During lockdown races were being cancelled or postponed continually until finally Scottish Athletics, the governing body for athletics in Scotland announced that races could commence from 1st August following Government Guidelines.

July 8th I was on an easy hill run and being complacent enjoying my running then I had yet another trip, landed with a hefty thud on my knee. My right knee took the brunt of it, I rolled around in agony for a while then eventually hauled myself up and hobbled home, finding it difficult to put any weight onto my leg. The next morning it was badly swollen and the day after so I had it X-Rayed to ensure that no bone damage had been done, a dislocated patella was the outcome! I laid off running for 10 days only going for walks until the pain and swelling subsided. I tested it on a jog / walk with a friend, thinking it would only be about 8 miles we extended it in search of the Covenaters Grave located the Pentland Hills, we ended up doing 15 miles, good knee test with no mishaps.

On Strava I am following a Carnethy Club runner, Jonny Muir, who set off on 2 July 2020 in an attempt to create a Round of the Pentlands which involved almost 51 miles with 13,041 ft elevation, excluding the Tumps, taking him only 12hrs 23mins. I was inspired by his adventuring over the Southern end of the Pentland's which I was not familiar with. There is a very interesting story about the legend of the Covenanters and The Battle of Rullion Green in the Pentland Hills. In 17th c. Scotland, a "Covenanter" was one who refused to accept the Church of Scotland, declaring allegiance to the Scottish Presbyterian Church. The name derives from their faithfulness to the National Covenant of 1643. The "Covenanters" would gather in secret in the hills and woodland for their own nightly services. If discovered, they were beaten, fined, imprisoned and often killed for their religious beliefs. A minister found preaching Covenanter views was subject to execution. A Covenanter army had risen in south-west Scotland and had advanced to Edinburgh to attempt to win support, while pursued by a Government army. The Government army finally caught up to them at Rullion Green, and defeated them on 28th November 1666, on the edge of the Pentland Hills. The Covenanter force of around

900 were met by around 3,000 soldiers. A battle ensued in which 100 Covenanters were reported killed on the field, and a further 300 as they tried to escape. Around 120 Covenanters were taken prisoner and sentenced to death. Many were executed in Edinburgh, but a number were sentenced to hang back in south-west Scotland as a warning to others against future risings. The memorial tombstone I was searching for is near the summit of Black Law, Scotland. The stone inscription reads: "SACRED to the Memory of A COVENANTER who fought and was wounded at Rullion Green, Nov 28th 1666 and who died at Oaken Bush the day after the Battle, and was buried here BY ADAM SANDERSON OF BLACKHILL." The shepherd, Adam Sanderson, answered a knock at his door to a severely wounded fugitive covenanter named John Carphin of Ayrshire. He refused to enter, knowing this could cause harm to the shepherd and his family "Bury me within sight of the Ayrshire hills" was his solemn request. The next day, Adam Sanderson found the Covenanter's body at Oaken Bush. Adam carried John up Black Law, burying him near the summit, granting him an everlasting view of the hills. A coded stone is said to have marked the spot. In 1841, the monument there today

was erected by the Minister of Dunsyre. The stone ruins of Adam Sanderson's Blackhill cottage can still be seen. Which I managed to locate whilst on another run. The grave was excavated by archaeologists who found the Covenanter's body wrapped in a red cloak . In the 1960's, the original old stone was discovered lying face down reading "A Covenanter / Dunsyre 1666". This original marker stone now sits in the Dunsyre Kirk, in Dunsyre, South Lanarkshire, Scotland.

The Covenanter Grave on Black Law

Scurry to the Sea 2020 was one of the first races, if not the first, to go ahead during Covid-19 restrictions. A lot of changes were put in place at the start and finish thought carefully out by Peter Ness, Race Director. I had entered the race and wanted to experience the new race structure we were about to enter. The knee had considerably improved which I tested by running up Allermuir Hill the day before to check how to avoid rocky terrain and trip hazards.

The race started with a short hill run to the top of Allermuir 1042ft in the Pentland Hill's then it was downhill all the way to the sea at Musselburgh. This covers a mixture of cross country, urban orienteering and road-running whilst navigating your way to the beach finish at Musselburgh. We had to follow the 2m rule and keep the distance at the start and finish area (and where practical throughout). This was following a sportif style individual start with no mass start. As we were all self-starting the time only started when we activated our dibbers at the start line. The race used these electronic contactless dibbers as a C19 test, passing 3 dibber points at CK1, 2 and 3 and then a final dibber crossing the finish-line. When you activated your dibber, it lit up on your wrist to confirm you contacted the point.

I was slotted into Group A with the following

pattern similar to groups B & C

8.15am - 8.30am - Arrive and register (staying 2m apart in the line)
8.45am – 8.50am - Join the start line queue (staying 2m apart in the line)
8.50am - Starter horn was a beep every 4 seconds thereafter.

The race went as planned, running not racing and no further mishaps along the way, including the short cut of hopping over the wall, at a garage, climbing the tree to aid assistance. I was only 20 mins slower than previous years and no further damage done to my knee.

There was no Prize Giving under the current restrictions at the finish line. After crossing the finish-line we kept moving down 2 separate taped corridors, where we removed the dibbers and placed in a box. There were tables to pick up your Scurry to the Sea t-shirt along with a banana and Active Root to rehydrate. As I was waiting on friends, I had to move around the beach to watch out for them, not being allowed to congregate together.

I was/we were waiting on an announcement from the London Marathon to say it will be postponed until April 2021, training for it had not entirely gone to plan with all the injuries I had suffered. The email landed, from Hugh Brasher, Race director, still not announcing anything instead advising us to await another e-mail! They advised on their operations over the past month, how they had been working closely with the Department for Digital, Culture, Media & Sport, the Mayor's Office, UK Athletics, the Royal Parks, the emergency services and their many partners in London to show how the London Marathon could socially distance on Sunday 4 October. However, there were areas requiring further consultation with local NHS Trusts, the emergency services and local authorities which means they were still unable to confirm their plans for another 10 days. Then the announcement came: -

"I am sad to announce that we cannot hold the London Marathon in the way that has happened every year since 1981. The health and safety of our runners, our charities, our sponsors, our volunteers, our medics, our communities and our city is always our priority.

Therefore, we cannot embark on that intensely personal journey from Blackheath to Buckingham Palace, with the crowd cheering us on, with the gods of our sport leading the way, running together in mind, body and spirit with tens of thousands of people.

We understand that for many of you this news is hugely disappointing, though for some of you it may be a relief to have certainty about what is happening on Sunday 4 October."

It was a relief for me as I had not continued with training as I had foreseen it would not go ahead and I was quite happy to defer my entry to a future London Marathon. There was the opportunity to run a virtual London Marathon on Sunday 4 October 2020 to help the charities with desperately needed fundraising. To run from 00:00 to 23:59:59 BST on Sunday 4 October to complete your 26.2 miles and earn a finisher medal and finisher T-shirt for The 40th Race for a fee of £20. Although unique I am content to wait until 3rd October 2021 to run my 16th London Marathon.

More interesting on the same day, the very best marathoners of all time, including Eliud Kipchoge, Kenenisa Bekele, Brigid Kosgei, Manuela Schär and David Weir, will race on a closed loop course around St James' Park, under the UK government's current rules for Elite Sport. Other elite athletes from around the world will be trying to gain Olympic qualification. The BBC ran extensive coverage featuring the elite races.

During these challenging months the world has suffered from the impacts of Covid-19, it is a change, a huge change, and we endured so much change over the last year. The options of virtual races started to swamp the race calendars.

7 MEDIA ARTICLES

BBC News Online: -
'I was paralysed but a year on I'm running a mountain marathon'
By Angie Brown
BBC Scotland News

A year ago Carole Fortune was lying on her bedroom floor having collapsed as she got out of bed.

She had suffered a stroke which left half her body paralysed. All she could do was shout for her daughter to call an ambulance.

Little did the 56-year-old know she would be attempting to run a challenging mountain marathon just 12 months later.

Speaking at her home in Edinburgh, Carole said she initially thought she had just overdone it at the gym the night before.

"I had absolutely no pain but then I noticed I couldn't move my arm or my leg and that's when I knew it was serious and I knew I had had a stroke, the mother-of-two said.

"My daughter Jade could see my mouth was down on one side.

"I was completely numb down my left side and all my strength on that side was completely gone. It was terrifying."

At the hospital Carole was asked if she wanted to have a dangerous clot busting treatment called thrombolysis, which involves a strong drug being administered intravenously.

She said: "They said it is a very potent drug

which could either kill me or cure me.

"I said 'Give me the drug because I don't want to be paralysed for the rest of my life'.

"Within about half an hour doctors could see in my face that I already looked better as my facial droop had lifted.

"Then I noticed I could lift my left arm a little and I waved to my children at the end of the bed."

She still felt very weak though and her mind was racing about whether she would be able to run again.

The Gala Harriers runner had done 15 London Marathons, having always qualified for a Good For Age place. One year she won an elite London Marathon place which meant running from the same pen as three times London Marathon winner, Paula Radcliffe.

She said: "I was panicking over whether I would be able to run ever again and asked the doctors if they thought I would be able to run the London Marathon six months later.

"They said I had a good chance of recovery because I was so fit before my stroke."

So once she had left the hospital she started trying to walk. She went for gruelling physiotherapy sessions and speech therapy.

Once she was confident she could walk for three miles unaided she started trying to jog little sections.

She said: "I was scared to go out by myself because I thought I would have another stroke. I made sure I always had someone with me for support. I felt apprehensive and aware of how weak my body was.

"I felt clumsy because one side of my body was working normally but the other side was much weaker and so I felt off balance."

Despite having several falls where she dislocated her knee cap, fractured her rib, cut her eye open and smashed her expensive running watch, Carole persevered.

"There was never any question in my mind of me giving up on my running," she said. "I didn't even think about that when I was all battered and bruised from falling."

When the London Marathon 2020 was cancelled for a second time on Sunday 4 October due to coronavirus restrictions, Carole has now decided to run a marathon over the mountains on the same day instead.

The route will take her from her house in Edinburgh at Robert Louis Stevenson's path Cockmylane to Black Mount Parish Church in Dolphinton in Lanarkshire and involves almost 5,000ft of climbing. She will be raising money for Chest Heart and Stroke Scotland.

Although Carole's left side is still weaker than her right, she has been building herself up to run long distances again and says she will resort to crawling rather than giving up on her 26.2 miles challenge on the day.

She will tap into the strength of recovery she found when she was knocked off her bike by a car in 2009 on the Moffat Road in the Scottish Borders, which led to her having operations for a broken neck and fractured skull.

She said: "My friend who is a nurse said it is unbelievable that I'm running a marathon so soon after a stroke, which makes me feel happy. I've come so far and the last year has been a huge journey."

Lawrence Cowan, director of fundraising at **Chest Heart and Stroke Scotland**, said: "Carole is an inspiration. To be taking on such a difficult challenge, and especially after having a stroke just a year ago is incredible.

"Carole is the embodiment of no life half lived and that's what Chest Heart & Stroke Scotland is all about. We want people to do more than survive after a stroke, we want them to really live."

Chest Heart Stroke Scotland (CHSS) published the following:-

Marathon mum wants to raise a 'Fortune' after stroke

A year ago Carole Fortune from Edinburgh was lying on her bedroom floor paralysed after having a massive stroke. But now she's running a marathon to give back to the charity that changed her life.

When Carole Fortune woke up on the floor unable to move, she didn't know what had happened to her.

Her first thought was that she had overdone things in the gym the night before, but she soon realised that she had no feeling down her left side.

It was terrifying

Full of panic she shouted on her daughter who quickly realised that her mum was having a stroke and called 999.

"I woke up on my bedroom floor and couldn't push myself up," explains Carole. "I knew something was seriously wrong when I had no feeling at all in my left arm and leg, it was terrifying."

But luckily Carole's daughter Jade came to her rescue and spotted the signs of stroke straight away.

"I was so relieved that my daughter Jade was in the house when this happened as she often stays with her boyfriend at the weekends," says Carole. "I don't know what I would have done if she wasn't home. She could clearly see that my face had drooped and knew I was having a stroke."

My stroke floored me

Carole worked harder than ever before to get her strength back after stroke. "My stroke completely floored me and I have had to rebuild my strength from using furniture to walk with to being able to run again," she says.

"I recovered well because I was in good shape and thankfully got to hospital quickly which definitely improved my chances.

"Physically I was getting better but mentally I was still struggling as I was afraid and scared of another stroke occurring."

Thankfully, she started to get help from Chest Heart & Stroke Scotland's Stroke Nurse Thomas Jones. Thomas started visiting Carole regularly and was able to help and support her when she felt at her lowest.

Stroke nurse is brilliant

"After you have a stroke, your head is swimming with questions and so many worries and I was suffering from a lot of anxiety," says Carole.

"Thomas was absolutely brilliant. He helped me come to terms with this major thing that had just interrupted my life. He is so knowledgeable and answered all my questions I had about my stroke."

Carole is tackling the virtual London Marathon just one year on from suffering a paralysing stroke.

Thomas still supports me

"Since the stroke, I have struggled with my voice. I found that I spoke too fast and I couldn't help saying too much in one sentence then I was gasping for air.

"I couldn't speak loudly or clearly, making it difficult for me to join in conversations. Thomas arranged speech therapy sessions and the exercises helped with my confidence," explains Carole.

"He also arranged physiotherapist sessions as I have a weakness in my left shoulder girdle and that gave me exercises to strengthen it. I still struggle from time to time in certain situations with anxiety, but Thomas still supports me."

The charity that changed my life

A year on from her stroke, Carole is now taking on a massive physical challenge for Chest Heart & Stroke Scotland.

"It's now been a year since I faced the biggest challenge of my life, recovering from my stroke, and I'm determined to give back to the charity that changed my life," says Carole.

"That's why I decided to challenge myself to run the virtual London Marathon to help other stroke survivors like me. Not only is it 26.2 miles it has almost 5,000 ft elevation as I am running over the Pentland Hills to Dolphinton.

"I hope as many people as possible donate what they can, so that Chest Heart & Stroke Scotland can still be there for people like me who really need their help and services."

Donate to Carole's incredible marathon challenge and help others who desperately need our help right now.

The Daily Star Newspaper published the
following:-

'I'm fighting fit a year on from stroke'

by STEPHEN DEAL

A SUPER fit runner who had a stroke aged just 55 which left her paralysed is training for a marathon – just a year later.

Carole Fortune was found on her bedroom floor unable to move by her daughter in October last year.

She knew immediately what was happening as she was paralysed down her left hand side, and terrified daughter Jade, 24, could see her mum's face had drooped.

Jade dialled 999 and her mum was taken to hospital and given drug thrombolysis – which could have either caused a fatal haemorrage or saved her life.

Within 45 minutes of being given the 'miracle blood clot buster', her face had returned to normal and she was able to wave at Jade and younger child Ryan, 16, from her bed at the Royal Infirmary of Edinburgh – and she was released two days later.

Carole was terrified of going out by herself, but she was determined not to let the experience get the better of her and she is now training for the virtual London Marathon on October 4, on a route from the Pentland hills to Dolphinton in South Lanarkshire.

Carole said: 'I was in Lanzarote doing a volcanic run and I fell and cut my leg, which needed stitches, and I came home three weeks later.

'I lost a lot of blood and I had a four and a half hour flight home. It was never proved that was the reason but I'm convinced I had a blood clot.

'I was in bed and I must have turned to get out of bed, and I found myself on the bedroom floor, I tried to push myself up but I couldn't.

'I had to shout for my daughter, I couldn't get up off the floor.

'It was a full stroke, I was paralysed down my left side and couldn't move my left hand, arm or leg.'

Next weekend's event will be her 16th London Marathon and her 42nd in total. Carole said: 'I'm going to get my life back.'

In October it was World Stroke Day. CHSS (Chest Heart Stroke Scotland) contacted me as they were "looking at doing some press around World Stroke Day on 29th October and we were thinking about highlighting the FAST message (Face, Arm, Speech, Time) and it came to me that your story was a great example of the FAST message as your daughter had reacted so quickly to your stroke."

The story was in Edinburgh Evening News on page 3, the online page below and Grampian online.

https://www.edinburghnews.scotsman.com/health/hero-daughter-saves-mothers-life-after-she-suffered-life-threatening-stroke-edinburgh-home-3017537

https://www.grampianonline.co.uk/news/act-fast-if-you-suspect-a-stroke-and-dial-999-216548/

The final media article was on the 4th October 2020:- The Real People magazine published a story with a more light hearted approach.

ABOUT THE AUTHOR

Carole Fortune lives in Edinburgh with her two children, Jade age 24 and Ryan age 17 she continues to run, swim and take part in events.